AGENDA

Weatherings

Registered Charity Number: 326068

ISBN 978-1-908527-46-2

Published by

AGENDA AND EDITIONS CHARITABLE TRUST

General Office: Harts Cottage, Stonehurst Lane, Five Ashes, Mayfield, East Sussex TN20 6LL
Tel: 01825 831994   e-mail: editor@agendapoetry.co.uk

Submissions plus a brief biography should be sent via **email only** to
submissions@agendapoetry.co.uk
(see website for details and for opening of submissions window)

SUBSCRIBE ONLINE AT

www.agendapoetry.co.uk

Subscription queries to: admin@agendapoetry.co.uk

Or cheques (payable to *Agenda*): Harts Cottage, Stonehurst Lane, Five Ashes,
Mayfield, East Sussex TN20 6LL   Tel: 01825 831994

Subscription rates

Inland
Private £28   Concessions (students/OAPs) £22   Libraries and Institutions £35

Europe
Private £30 (€35)   Libraries and Institutions £45 (€50)

Overseas
Private £35 (US$46)   Libraries and Institutions £50 (US$62)

Vol 55   No 1–2   Winter/Spring 2022

AGENDA

CONTENTS

POEMS

REVIEWS OF TRANSLATIONS

CHOSEN BROADSHEET POET

NOTES FOR BROADSHEET POETS

FOUR POEMS FOR UKRAINE

In memoriam Grey Gowrie (1939-2021)

Agenda would like to express its sincere gratitude to Lord Grey Gowrie for his loyal support which enabled *Agenda* to keep going over many decades.

When the tide comes in...

'When the tide comes in, I'll marry you'...
Did you hear the nibs of all the girls
I taught moving, out of time, over

their ruled pages, composing poems
for you from that first line of yours?
They are still at it, loops and curves

blurred with ink blots from your pen
as your voice echoes down corridors
to the bounce of fluted green skirts.

Did you hear, at news of your death,
birds, too, singing your lines backwards
as if wanting to migrate to all the lives

you lived, with your many callings.
And the sales girls in Biba advising
the era's dusky-pink maxi dresses,

the suede platform boots, thigh-high,
duck-egg blue outfits, feather boas,
every till ringing for whoever

you fancied. So much I heard from you
over the phone in what was your last year:
tomes you were reading: *The Decline*

and Fall of the Roman Empire; your love
of Chaucer, the workings of Christies.
And, in tender tones, how you met,

over a kitchen table in Austria,
Neiti, your exquisite real-life princess.
So much to discuss: your poems, mine...

your voice so spirited, youthful
as you jokingly suggested you might be
a 'telephone pest'. All the while

I had no idea you were bed-ridden:
your noble head, acute mind, no trace
of self-pity while your frail body shrank

into the bed-linen...Yes, the sale
of your London House, a relief –
and I must come down to Wales

so you can show me around, horses
in the near distance, mountains beyond.
Now I think this poem a gift from you,

not me, as you put the pen in my hand,
the schoolgirls, grown into muses,
chorusing how, when the tide comes in,

goes out, out and in, they'll marry you.
Dear Grey, despite your demesnes,
your charmed urbane-ness, your need

always of a chauffeur, no good with wheels –
I will keep stoked the turf-fire
in the Delgany we both knew

that smouldered forever in your heart.

Patricia McCarthy

(This poem appeared in the recent issue of *The London Magazine* to whom thanks are owed for permission to re-print it).

In memoriam Thomas Kinsella (1928 – 2021)

Amen, I Said

The Tree of Idleness

The evening light was grey, diminishing;
the lower sky a rough-sand wallpaper, and above
dark apricot; the hissing promenade lamps
just lighting up. We had parked the car by the low kerb,
stood in salt air a moment, listening;
the sea stirred softly, this day's shoreline shambles
to be guessed at in the dusk; I prayed this evening
be an ocean without turbulence.

Eleanor and Tom were waiting by the door;
a welcoming light, warm and dim, shone from within
and a pinched, out-of-place palm tree
hung despondent fronds. We were seated in our places
ceremoniously, amid delicate scents
of fresh bread baked; snow-flake soft white napkins
with all the settings in order, cutlery
and plate, and high-cut glistening crystal.

We talked of the familiar, of belief and unbelief,
of the main mystery
not to be understood. We drank Cypriot white wine
and red, warm and russet-deep, from Greece. Eleanor
kept watch on our conversation, while offering Tom
sparkling water... and I felt that sorrow, old
insistent pecking bird, was driven away this little while.

A copper stoup with lemon segments
floating in scented water,
offered cleansing as we rose, claimed
coats and scarves and went out into the night. High
over the darkness of the sea were the wild
prairies of the stars, with the planet Mars –
damaged russet-red fruit – holding close to earth,
and why did I think of Mahler, the tenor voice insisting
Dunkel ist das Leben, ist der Tod.

We parted, in renewed affection. And I watched the blood-red
tail-lights of the car as they turned away towards the hills
of Wicklow. Master, I prayed, *sláinte*, your health,
and may the compassionate hands of the Christ sustain you.

Fair Eleanor...

The first frosts of autumn had laid
a patina of white across the grasses, like dust
scattered on delicate leaves of the briar rose; soon
the blooms themselves would be brown and drooping.
The usual noises were heard across the suburbs,
a little muted, and not distracting; he sat,
head in his hands, in self-devouring prayer,
mind – long trained in reasoned thought,
in careful ordering of notes and calm rehearsal –
focused: but nothing stirred, the sureties that had ghosted
his lines and days and the sustaining presence
of a steady love, had fled away. Moralities.
Mortality. Flesh with its burthens of vein and blood.
Music flowed in the room, steady, and a stream
unsettled: *Mein Herz ist müde... Ja, gib mir Ruh'.*
For the time being, up on the bookshelves, the small
urn; waiting; watchful. There would be a way
to find life again, to hold firm for the time remaining.
After long suffering the heart wearies;
tonight, at rare moments, the light appeared to flicker,
filling the dark corners with darker presences; *fair*

Eleanor, he had written, *o Christ thee save*. He knew
a radical pity still for the Christ, that intense gaze,
critical and caring, compassionate yet precise
in judgment, too direct for this world. And yet
there will be time, and more, to rest, at peace within
the ultimate essence. From the player, the sharp
soprano voice was lifting to a dread despair, before
dropping back to quiet, unresolved, yet beautiful.

Messenger: at the Edge

… a way to make in the world

That afternoon the whole Atlantic Ocean
flooded the wide basin of the bay,
cathedral sea-cliffs and buttresses, the mountain's
embracing arms on the far edge, here the frustration
of the waters, urgent against
the piled-up-stones and boulders of the shore;

enormous seas off land had tumbled up
heaving waters on Dookinella strand, churning, then –
the waves spent – spread out lolling across the sand;

threatening clouds loomed over us, poor
puny humans, who were at play together in the garden
at the back of the house.

Freshly cooked crab claws, the flesh
grainy white and wholesome
as we cracked the shells on large shore-stones
and shared beers and wine,
dipping the claws in a bitter-lemon and pickle relish,
Atlantic sounding from the bay, the sky holding.

*

Kinsella:

     poet of disillusion, grief and loss:
     poet of spirit and of truth,
in wisdom earned through suffering, absences, le petit mal,
     dismissing the spurious, instigating order;
          Hermes, Mercury, the winged sandals of the Christ,
transcribing messages between mortals and the gods –
    a thumb crooked by the telegram pouch,
        shoes polished, and a way to make in the world.

        *

Achill: the island; a local crowd, honoured
and honouring, a rare reading of his poems
by Thomas Kinsella, the poet Mahon standing by
in case...It was a strong, convincing voice
clarifying the disorderly matter of human needs.
So the afternoon *(In dem Häuschen sitzen Freunde...*
trinken, plaudern) was celebration. Under the sound
of coming thunder, we took shelter in the house
by a middling turf fire. Too soon, Tom was
stuttering, his hands shook, his face had gone
a sodden greyish white...and Eleanor hushed us
quickly out while she cared for him. I watched
a brazen great black-backed gull come picking
at the bits of shell scattered across the grass,
that baleful eye, that bitter-lemon snapping bill.

        *

I was standing outside Hanna's bookshop window,
Nassau Street in Dublin, and suddenly Tom
was standing by me, in greatcoat, carrying

a neat brown-leather briefcase. 'Ah, Tom. . .'
'John. Well met. And how are you?' 'Great,'
I answered, 'everything going well.' He seemed

to flinch, stood back, and said: 'Oh dear! John, I'm
sorry put your head down, the bricks are in the air.'
The intense and caring gaze: the gentleman, poet,

for whom the poem is enough. And is never enough.

A Handful of High Grass

We dithered softly at the chapel door, late
afternoon, the light fading. It was December, the Birth
close at hand.
                        He came in state; the hearse,
coming slowly up the long avenue, breathed softly,
taking him out of the traffic
into this quietest of cities. We waited, masked still
and keeping distance. I felt his poems
stiffen in my breast, sorrow catching
at the heart.
                        It was farewell; the Victorian Chapel,
stone walls and tablets of cold stone, but I dreamed
a funeral march, drums slow-beating, high strings
muted.
            The words of grief and loss were warm, his final
podium lit and cherishing; in my mind I heard his words:
there is nothing to be done – only record.
Until the slow and disconcertingly silent sliding shut
of the curtains: Amen, I said, Amen.
                                                At home
Ursula and I raised a glass, the precisely
chiselled crystal, the old-gold richness of the whiskey:
to Eleanor and Tom, the real thing...

                                    *

We drove, bright January noon-time, up
the Military Road over the mountains, and out across
the upland commonage, the fells, the bog
cuttings with small and scattered clamps
of turf; there were streams, swift and sluggish
through fern and heather moorland, the white-wool
bog cotton, the bitter yellow iris – and then
Glenmacnass, the waterfall, scattered rocks
and boulders, the flung froth and spray, constant
unmusical but pleasing, plashing sound,
the water easing down along the lush valley.
Easy, on these age-old slopes, in a soft breeze,
to hear pipe music, lament or threnody, even

the skirling growl of chanters under the slip-jig
fingers of Littlebody, and his measling cry:
We'll meet again when I dance on your ashes. The urn
on the bookcase; the second urn. The mingled
ashes lifted on a scented breeze over the purple
buds of the heathers, settling softly, softly,
among the roots in old Irish soil. *Amen,* I said,
dear Eleanor, dear Tom, amen, o Christ, our Christ,
amen. By the time we turned for home
the evening chilled, the moon already white
over the city. Through the fir-trees I glimpsed
the cautious and precise stepping of a great-
antlered stag, quickly lost in darkness. The waterfall
was a ghostly white, grey mist rising to the night.

Still ist mein Herz...
    Master: auf Wiedersehen.

And until then –
    Farewell.

John F. Deane

In memoriam Brendan Kennelly (1936-2021)

Dear Brendan

i

Dear Brendan, I can still hear
your lilting voice on the telephone
that last time when your old head,
you said, was not that good any more.

I think I detected a stutter of fear
as away, it seemed, you were flown
with the fairies to a kind of homestead
where nothing could ever again be sure

in Listowel. Yet where your native tongue,
whose *fadas* and *buailtes* had merged
with your adopted English, the polyphony

was the pride of all the bells ever rung.
And the Atlantic and Irish seas surged
from the bedrock of epiphany.

ii

Dear Brendan, put a sheaf
of your own poems in your hand
and you'd recite eloquently by heart
their many voices, yourself their home.

Now you dump the fairies with relief –
back in your old College stomping ground,
Professor of every conceivable art,
your Darkest Fathers unearthed from loam.

Your corkscrew curls dance with you
past Bewleys, down Grafton Street
to the tune of 'On Raglan Road'

that you sang to me once. I knew
Death, for you, could never be a defeat,
dear Brendan, with all that life you showed

in your after-life veins, the wind your scribe
for new poems on sheets of tabled tides.

iii

Dear Brendan,
no more letters from you,
mentoring, praising
in that distinctive handwriting –
saved in bundles now,
their black Quink ink faded
down the decades
to the rust of dried blood.
No more Butlers chocolates
from Dublin, more recent
with shorter inscriptions
in the same Parker fountain pen.
The sea is your inkwell now,
filling itself with blue-black,
turquoise inks for you to dip into
when the wind is on retreat.
Foghorns announce your return
in a cloak of bird-feathers dropped
by the murmurations you described.
Know, Brendan, I will collect
your epistles from the water
and send them back
to where, divilishly courteous,
you forever resound.

Patricia McCarthy

Introduction

Welcome to this Weatherings issue of *Agenda*. I am sure we are all feeling weathered in one way or another, what with the pandemic and the turmoil in this country and elsewhere. And of course with the very recent loss of three great poets: Grey Gowrie, Thomas Kinsella and Brendan Kennelly

Honouring those three, the elegiac tone seems to run through these pages; the mystery of death and how to live here on earth – which we have all been up against more than ever recently – is probably the mainspring of all the best poetry and such poets manage to tease words out of what remains mostly wordless in order to communicate musically what can't often be put into normal speech. However, there is celebration also, touches of Spring with its new buds, crocuses, snowdrops and early primroses – and I hope readers enjoy the mix.

Agenda, as always, avoids following fashion or trends, and always aims to emphasise that it is the quality of the poetry that matters, irrespective of the poet's ethnicity, gender or awards such as prizes. Surely a poem should stand on its own, irrespective of the author.

There has always been a tradition in *Agenda* to give space to the long poem and here I have done just that: interspersed long poems or sequences with more compact poems so that the reader can dip in and out of whatever type of poem they fancy.

At the end of the day, a phrase of Philip Larkin's comes to mind: 'What will survive of us is love'. It is love that reprieves us all finally.

*   *   *

I wrote the above introduction five weeks or so ago, and now the world has turned upside down as we are three and a half weeks into the war in Ukraine – apocalyptic times. This war is on all our minds and it is hard to find words for all the suffering and loss.

Poetry and history-making, it seems, have always been intertwined in Ukraine. The country's political upheavals, from the Maidan Revolution to Russia's annexation of Crimea and the war in Donbas, have made bold, direct poetry particularly prominent. The following poem, by one of Ukraine's best-loved poets, **Serhiy Zhadan**, translated by John Hennessy and Ostap Kin – although presumably written before the present war – is particularly resonant today.

So I'll talk about it

So I'll talk about it:
about the green eye of a demon in the colorful sky.
An eye that watches from the sidelines of a child's sleep.
The eye of a misfit whose excitement replaces fear.
Everything started with music,
with scars left by songs
heard at fall weddings with other kids my age.
The adults who made music.
Adulthood defined by this – the ability to play music.
As if some new note, responsible for happiness,
appears in the voice,
as if this knack is innate in men:
to be both hunter and singer.
Music is the caramel breath of women,
tobacco-scented hair of men who gloomily
prepare for a knife-fight with the demon
who has just crashed the wedding.
Music beyond the cemetery wall.
Flowers that grow from women's pockets,
schoolchildren who peek into the chambers of death.
The most beaten paths lead to the cemetery and water.
You hide only the most precious things in the soil –
the weapon that ripens with wrath,
porcelain hearts of parents that will chime
like the songs of a school choir.
I'll talk about it –
about the wind instruments of anxiety,
about the wedding ceremony as memorable
as entering Jerusalem.
Set the broken psalmic rhythm of rain
beneath your heart.
Men that dance the way they quench
steppe-fire with their boots.
Women that hold onto their men in dance
like they don't want to let them go to war.
Eastern Ukraine, the end of the second millennium.
The world is brimming with music and fire.
In the darkness flying fish and singing animals give voice.
In the meantime, almost everyone who got married then has died.

In the meantime, the parents of people my age have died.
In the meantime, most heroes have died.
The sky unfolds, as bitter as it is in Gogol's novellas.
Echoing, the singing of people who gather the harvest.
Echoing, the music of those who cart stones from the field.
Echoing, it doesn't stop.

Also relevant, in a strange, parallel sense, to what is happening now are the two essays/reviews by Martyn Crucefix and David Cooke of translated works. Hence readers might like to turn to these first. Martyn reviews Durs Grunbein and Ulrike Almut Sandig, both translated by Karen Leeder, and David reviews Peter Huchel, translated by Martyn Crucefix.

Let's hope that, by the time this Weatherings issue of *Agenda* reaches the doors of subscribers that peace will so thankfully have been restored.

Patricia McCarthy

Peter Dale

Elegy of Elegies

I was at school when mother died.
I broke my fountain-pen in shock
when the news struck. I never cried.

(Her varicose ulcer and thrombosis.)
I made myself a silent vow
that nothing else would I allow,
ever to hurt as much as this.

It was a secret vow I kept,
whatever happened, for seventy years.
My wife's death let loose the tears —
dead on the kitchen floor, and I wept.

Yet seventy years of elegies,
this life-driven gift for language
that just prolonged the mourning anguish
for family, friends, contemporaries.

It needs massive blank megaliths,
anonymous to take as read
to mark all past and present deaths
while carved inscriptions erode to myths.

David Harsent

from *SKIN*

Jenny Haniver

Find her in dream, unnatural, feather and fin, eyes the colour
of sea, colour of sky, her gift to you your own name
spoken as if you could own it, tide-drift, wind-drift
bringing you to a soundless, sightless vacancy, freefall,
deep-dive, air and water forcing one another as you strike
the edge of night, blind and deaf and lost but still alive.

Stepping out of the shower, water to air, pearled, soft-
eyed, she is numbed by memory: how her fear
of falling is also a fear of drowning... Your face by hers
in the mirror, too near, too soon – she hasn't yet
found the full depth of her fall which might
never come if you lay hands on her like that.

Crucis

Grunewald: Unterlinden Museum

It is to put the torn body of God-made-man in open view,
webbed and spoiled, it is to offer him as trophy, to start a lurch
of lust in all who stand as if at the foot of the cross, it is
to witness their laughter, their slow dance hand in hand,
which gives them sight of the hanged man's ragged back,
gives sight of his shuttered face against a gathering sky.

Your lover is on her way. She has packed for a journey.
Your lives deflect and collide like broken paths in a wood
where you make a slow dance hand in hand as you must
and lose the ghost of the dance. This is the cost: to touch
and turn away, to be featureless, to go by another name.
It is why you wait for her in a place of love and pain.

Freggio

Silence shelves in the room, hard-edged. Dawn comes
as a palimpsest, stark-white, faces drawn and deleted.
She sleeps; you watch. What do you think of her –
that she's held in night-long dispute with the Bitch Goddess,
that she breathes in time with wave-break,
that she'll wake to an unexplained version of herself?

She breathes with the sea and wakes to downpour rain
shaping the window. No gain in that. Her dreams
lie skin-deep; you'll find them with a fingertip. The Goddess
came and went leaving on her a wound she now protects
with a close-cupped hand. That ragged sound is birdsong:
some tell in the rise and fall you'll never understand.

Patrick Wright

Winter Ghazal

Over bed covers of snow, I go in search of your eyes.
As the sun funnels through the glaze, in dreams I never
find your eyes. A new day without you. So, I caress your
pillow's furrow, a rivulet that carries my scent to your
half-moon eyes. I inspect marks on my flesh, hashtags
of ruffled sheets, temporary tattoos I can't bear to lose.
In the mind's eye, I bag your fingernail & wipe lipstick
off the mirror. As the sun fingers your fabrics, I learn
to revive your eyes. On waking this morning, I hear a
music box melody. Like you're a phantom limb, I feel
you still, your eyes, our clinch, our skin-to-skin. I cling
to your sarong, slung over a hook, untouched. How I
was braille under your eyes. & Kim, the wicker screen
is filtering light, it falls on the sill, on your gift of the
angel harp – & how you'd smile at this.

Anniversary

The season assails me: flashbacks – daffodils linked
with nausea, pinks of cherry blossom fallen
in my stomach's pit, the sickness of spring evocations ...

Like surgical gauze left behind, hurt comes in waves –
the burn of how we abandon each other.
When our film clips are stitched everything is vaudeville.

Skinless I drift through the manicured beds
through bluebells by the haunted parsonage.
I ask, 'God, what do all the symbols mean?' –

robins that land on benches, distant ice-cream vans'
nostalgia. Everything a beautiful catastrophe.
The rays of May penetrate. Spring blossoms,

torn crate paper ready for decoupage. As if the body's
stasis chamber knows the date –
anniversaries through springtime, through springtime ...

Are we on pause or between sentences?
'Acceptance' is a word like the cigarette scar on my arm –
the scar my watch face hides.

The mind says it's create or die – create or die.
I cling to our love like a rodeo. I write your lines
sous rature. And still, we are star-crossed:

you on your side, me on mine.

Jane Lovell

Clematis

The clematis survives you,
battened to the wall as it is
with wire and bamboo canes.

Its buds, like pale lamps,
could be almost triumphant
if they dared.

Bedded in soil, I find small slabs
of stone protecting the roots.
You should be buried here.

Maybe your ashes will find
their way back home
riding an evening breeze,

and settle, unnoticed,
to be washed by the rain
deep into the earth.

Next year's blooms
would have an air about them,
a pride,

their petals bold against the sky,
holding their own
in this brittle light.

The Final Judgement

We end here.
Angels leave via the windows,
their lead-white wings defined by carbon.
Light fills the chapel with shadows.
Note your proximity to the fiery slope
and the Devil, grey ogre, feasting
on the undead.

Your Saviour sits above the cross,
hands outstretched in a mantle of gold.
His eyes are not on you – there is no point
in beseeching him with your gaze –
his focus is drawn to the distance,
at an angle that suggests sorrow.

Before you leave, take a moment
to consider the presence of azurite
and mixite, the ultramarine heavens
pinned by gold leaf stars.
Already traces of arsenic and lead
settle in the pits of my bones.

Remember me here, high on this platform,
a brush between my teeth,
my one good eye judging the depth
and distance, giving you Heaven
and Hell in an instant, drawing you in
to ponder your own demise.

Vitulus

i

He suckled. He grazed.
Grasses, buttercups, a mash of nameless leaves
and stems foaming on his eely tongue.
He had the whole Sky as his mother,
the Earth as his soul.

ii

The blade works from throat to tail:
spill and tumble, organs a muddle of bloody parcels
unfolding onto stone, slick and remote.

His tongue hangs from the slack jaw.
How his eyes show shock and sky
in their shine.

iii

We soak the skin in lime, prod it down with staffs.
It rises and looms, settles.
Our eyes smart and burn in the haze.

Eight days gone, we haul out its pale slap,
nail it to a frame, scrape the last fine hairs away.
A skim of fat gathers on the blade.

Limed and scudded, the pelt dries and stiffens;
a map of paths wandering virgin terrain.

iv

The world is drawn inside your skin,
its pale parchment shrinking at light;
the endless raking of the lunellum remembered
in its translucence.

Undulations appear over time; a shift
in the landscape. A memory of green:
soilburst of shoots ruckling the meadow
below your hooves.

Note: The Hereford Mappa Mundi was drawn on a single calf skin.

Jeremy Hooker

Dutch Girl

i

Dearest, how
can you be 'late'
when your very absence
is my companion?

You are here
                        you are there
a woman by herself
musing in a room.
Is that my letter in your hand?

Alone, with maps on the wall,
you are a world.

ii

So close, so far
you bring your country
to me – the brick streets,
cycle paths and Saxon villages,
windmills & dykes,
a heron flying over
or stick-still among the reeds.
I recall such pleasure
with you, my love.

Clay & water & fire
were our elements,
all our senses alive
and most of all, touch.

iii

I think of the Waddenzee
and sand islands
with their cemeteries.
I see the fields of blue clay,
pasture that was sea
at the land's edge,
cattle and gulls
on salt grass at the marge.
It is all you, and not you.
There is more to see,
always – the rooms,
the streets, the tangible, elusive
now, not fading, only too far to reach.

iv

Martini Tour, 'the old grey one',
towered over us on days
at the Grote Markt, where,
in the crush of pedals, knees and feet
we would walk gingerly
around the stalls, where
men sliced cheese for us
to taste, and we bought
vegetables, fish, and fruit.
You would then load me
with shopping bags, string
biting into my fingers,
and we would walk home
laughing at my burden,
complete with happiness.

v

Winter brought skaters to ponds
in the Noorderplantsoen,
old and young together,
whole families – parents,
grandparents, children,
circling, falling, helping
each other up, red-faced
with exertion, bright-eyed,
shouting and laughing.

Once an ice storm silenced the city.
Birch trees bent like hoops
under the weight of ice.
Pylons like steel giants buckled at the knees.
When I opened the door
my beard and eyebrows froze.

Memory brings bitter cold.
But we were in the warm,
at the window together,
relishing the sublime emptiness
of silent streets, cars immobilized,
gables tusked with icicles.

vi

Often I return
to the Korreweg, not
the house only, on the corner
of Balistraat, but the life
to which you welcomed me.

I remember the garden
we climbed to, squirming
through a trap door
onto the roof – like being
born again in middle age.

And on the roof
                sunflowers,
and you bending over them
face to face, my lady
of the sunflowers.

Around us, spires,
clocktowers, smoke
from a factory,
houseboats and barges
on the canal,
a heron flying over –
        Groningen,
the city I came to love.

vii

Time paints me pictures,
landscapes and portraits,
meadows with cows and horses,
riotous families, contemplative
women, and faces, always faces,
often the same face, young and old.

Grave and wondering,
self-seeing, the artists of your land
look out of time, beyond
comings and goings
of generations, past loss and grief.
A time that is forever shines in their eyes.

Is that what memory can be?
Can our time live,
or must it be buried with the years?
I know the life we made
will be with me until I die.

Love isn't like a body
buried or given to the flames
but part of our very being
with a life after life
that, alas, we cannot touch.

Widower

He has gone walkabout
in the dim-lit hours,
peering in faces
of fellow patients
who are asleep, or wander
in landscapes of their own.
He alone is awake, crossing
the outback of a dream,
cast out to wander, peering
in each face for one face,
listening for the voice
that will tell him who he is.

David Cooke

How a Heart Breaks

i.m. Martin Cooke (1955-2021)

'Behold the fowls of the air'
                    Matthew 6:26

This is the way it happens: a voice on the phone
explaining that one we took for granted
is no longer there, that junk food
and countless pints which wrecked
your balance and strained your heart
became in the end too much –
even at your shuffling pace.

Refusing to put a penny aside, so long
as you could buy a drink, your hapless ways
endeared you to all: the ducking and diving
by which you survived, the crazy
pickles you got through.

Simply living from day to day,
you always heard what we were saying
but carried on your own way,
sustained by football, films and rock –
your knowledge of trivia
dazzling, your grasp of the past
decisive. In a house
of scholars you were a savant
in a different way. No fixtures,
albums or dates escaped you.

We bought our first records together:
I Feel Free and *Paper Sun* –
though the only match I've ever attended
was one I took you to.
Before you died you supplied
the details: Reading v Southend Utd,
with your team winning 4 – 2.

So farewell, Martin, at rest now,
surely, amongst the gentlest souls,
who never strove
or sowed dissension,
or stored up wealth in barns.

Peter Weltner

East Wind

after Du Mu, for Jason Wirth

This morning, just as the last red glow of dawn
turned golden, I passed an old Chinese woman
walking down a cracked sidewalk while bottle
brush trees, shedding their filaments and pollen
in the breeze, gently powdered her tight, tufted

jacket. She strolled steadily, meditatively,
silently, in no rush to go anywhere, formal,
masked, white haired, her head bowed low,
her hands clasped behind her bent, hunched back.
Her jacket was bird-beak black, slightly torn,

worn and plain but threaded with silver,
her beaded slippers orange and silken, her gray
slacks baggy. As we strolled past each other,
she nodded once, her eyes, in the burgeoning
sunshine, smiling with joy. I thought of ancient

Chinese screens as I observed her pass and fade
into the remains of night: their graceful cranes,
acorn-shaped mountains, tall cane, thin reeds,
streams, waterfalls, a fat monk in a wooden hut,
two women pole fishing, or a solitary poet in exile

with brush and ink pot composing, beneath pine
trees shadowing ravines and a rushing river, a poem
I imagine might be read in the afterlife, the paradise
of eternal moments seen in an ordinary day. It comes
to me how at each sunrise the world slips more out of sight

into pure light, like the old Chinese woman I watched walk
away this morning so slight she weighed on the earth
no more than the pollen and filament-slender petals borne
aloft by an east wind that fell on her noble stooped shoulders
as if she'd just been anointed with the last golden red dust of dawn.

Uru An-Na

The Milky Way consists of a hundred billion stars or more,
the number mind-numbing, of course, the distance
unthinkable. Where I stand alone, close to shore,
massive waves swell and crash with little resistance
from the cliffs. A big storm is due to hit just hours
from now, threatening to batter the coast with gale-force
winds, toppling trees, flattening dunes. The moon glowers
down on the surging sea, the sky still star-lit and unclouded.
It is unfathomable how ever-recurring-night rolls on and on
and yet changes as people must move in the land of the dead,
forever the same, yet restless and hovering, their lives never done
with. I stare up at the sky, searching for more signs of the storm
on its way. As I wait, I picture a constellation, now no more seen
in the heavens, the people who named it long gone, too. I imagine its form,
what myths it might have been given, what truths it was once said to mean.

ii

So Gilgamesh wanders the earth always, ever in search
of what he yearns for, something huge missing,
not just love, now that Enkidu's dead, but to reach
deep into the sea and to find what he needs, diving

into the ensuing flood of life, deep deep to the bottom,
to discover the plant, promised, that could be
his salvation, not his lover – no, not him,
not any more – but the flower of heartbeat, immortality

riddled with thorns and nettles that the sea monster,
the monstrous sea, all of it, snatches away
from his grip before he can taste it, high water
and winds whirling him in the storm, and he their prey

until back in Uruk, lives, ages later, as the last day's sun
slips behind his palace's gates, he sees rising
what Ptolemy will later name Orion,
in his tongue, Uru An-Na, hunter, bull-fighter, the light of heaven, undying.

Mary O'Donnell

Snowdrops

i.m. Bridget Coleman-O'Donnell

My grandmother took snuff,
and a daily egg straight from the shell.

Snowdrops travelled with her,
dug from the scattered Limerick farm

she left with her husband:
for Ballyneale, Coachford,

then, finally, Glaslough
and a crooked house above a quarry.

Three times she dug up,
three times she planted,

three times the tender roots
tasselled down and grew.

When she died, my father dug again,
lifting a clump for her grave.

They bloom now each February,
white and dip-headed, witness

to her journeys across fine fields,
spread wide as Bridget's cloak.

Common Time during the First Lockdown

He persuades me to try the duet:
Vaňhal's Sonata in B Flat Major for Clarinet
and Piano. I warn of my sight-reading,
the kind that once drew bruised knuckles
when the teacher whacked down
with her wooden pointer.
Somehow this evening isn't one
for practice, early summer has unloosed
the music from behind my eyes,
it travels straight to the ear,
where a fire is burning.
All I can hear is symphonic,
fern-greens and hellebore yellows,
or the pert tail of a pied wagtail
juddering like a bow where it plays the grass
in perfect pitch as sun sets, moon rises.

The Intimate Future

The first day will startle in a paradise
of spectacle and movement. In this release
from the wintry cocoon, the long chill
over, we will forget our solitude.
Like nectar-starved butterflies, we'll cluster
together in displays of brightening wings,
velvety trims, our chitined scales and spots
trembling at the end of long starvation.

We'll fly close – so close – to one another
in drifts of prismatic colour, our patterns,
shapes, antennae, colliding, shifting,
crowding sociably to drink and drink:
such intimate nectars, proboscis-fed
to another's need, wings sugar-drowsy.

Patricia McCarthy interviews David Harsent

David Harsent has published twelve volumes of poetry which have won numerous awards. Most recently, *Legion* won the Forward Prize. *Night* was triple short-listed in the UK and won the Griffin International Poetry Prize. *Fire Songs* won the T.S. Eliot Prize. A new collection, *Loss*, appeared in January 2020. *Salt Moon*, a collaboration with photographer Simon Harsent, and a pamphlet, *Homeland: Eighteen Bitter Songs*, versions of Yannis Ritsos, were published in 2021.

Harsent's writing for music and for the opera stage has involved collaborations with several composers, though most often with Harrison Birtwistle. Birtwistle/Harsent operas have been performed at major venues worldwide.

Harsent is a Fellow of the Royal Society of Literature and Fellow of the Hellenic Authors Society. He is Professor Emeritus at the University of Roehampton.

P McC: *David, as a very distinguished English poet, can you explain what started you off in your writing of poems? I remember you saying you didn't come from a literary family.*

DH: It's a long-ish story. My father was a bricklayer-labourer. My mother's side of the family was on the upper side of lower-middle-class. My maternal grandmother was twice widowed and scraped a living as the weekday-nights and all-day-Sunday telephone operator on the Post Office switchboard in a small mid-Bucks town. A three-bedroom flat came with the job. I lived there with my mother, my great grandmother, my grandmother and my aunt. When he returned from the war, my father joined us. I once went back to that flat with Hugo Williams, who was writing a piece about me for the *TLS*. He looked round the one sitting room, the kitchen, the three bedrooms, and said, 'Where did you all sleep?' To this day, I still don't know.

When I was nine, my parents were allocated a council house on an estate, though we always went back to the Post Office for Sunday lunch. The flat was on the high second floor of the building. There was a stone staircase that went down to a concrete floor. Two years later – I was eleven – lunch over, my aunt and I were leaving for Sunday School. I decided to slide down the banister, lost my balance, pitched over from the top rail, and fell down the stairwell – a twenty-five foot drop. My aunt rushed into the telephone exchange and told my grandmother who phoned the local doctor; he would call at the Post Office regularly to check on my great-grandmother's serial infirmities and my father's war-wounds, so knew the place – not least the staircase – well. He asked, 'Is he dead?' For a time after this, I had a quarrel with God, given that this had happened when I was on my way to chapel: so much for His caring for every hair of my head. I forgave the Almighty when I came to hear that, by rights, I should have died.

In fact, I was unharmed save for a concussion. No one could understand how I'd survived, let alone not broken my neck, back, legs. After a short stay in hospital, I spent time in bed, recovering from the concussion, at the Post Office flat; my grandmother was my nurse. There was no TV; the 'wireless' was in the living room. I had always read voraciously (and had frequently been chided for it). My grandmother went to the local library and brought back an armful of books. One of them was a sort of Bumper Book for Boys, with tales of Arctic exploration, of the conquests of Empire, dramatic biographies of 'heroes' like Baden-Powell and other such grotesques; but, between the stories were poems, all of the same sort, each telling of conflict, love, jealousy, betrayal, witchery, demonic possession and violent death. I could understand some, but not all, of it; I seem to remember that accounts of sexual shenanigans particularly caught my attention, though I wasn't quite sure why. I read the poems over and over. Finally, I asked my grandma to go back to the library and ask whether they had a book of such poems. She came back with Quiller-Couch's *Oxford Book of Ballads*. The Border Ballads. I never returned the book. From that time I never really wanted to do much else in the world than write poems. I'm still at it.

P McC: Which poets in those days inspired you?

DH: So, not so much poets as poems: 'Tam Lin', 'The Demon Lover', 'The Twa Corbies', 'Little Musgrave'…all of them. *A grave, a grave, Lord Barnard cried / To put these lovers in / But lay my lady on the upper hand / For she came of the nobler kin.* The rhythm of that four-beat, three-beat stanza was in my head day and night.

P McC: And did you have any mentors?

DH: Given my background, I didn't, as a child, know anyone who might have encouraged me. I didn't go to university: it wasn't for the likes of us, really. My fall meant I hadn't taken the 11-plus. I passed the 13-plus and my father decided I should go to a Technical rather than Grammar School: that *was* for the likes of us. The headmaster was a war-time appointee, ignoramus, Philistine, a brayer and a flogger who, because no new teacher stayed at the school for more than a couple of terms, was left with (apart from one man) a staff no less ignorant, ill-qualified and brutal than he. I left, aged sixteen, and went to work in a bookshop.

In my early twenties, having twice been declared homeless, I was living, with my wife and two small children in a two-up, two-down terraced cottage with no bathroom and an outside privy. We lived there for six years.

My elder son was born there. We were bone-achingly poor; sometimes I stole to buy food. I was writing poems and sending them to the usual mags and journals. Those that were rejected by the *Observer*, went to the *Review*; those that came back from the *Review* went to the *TLS*, those back from the *TLS* to the *New Statesman*, and so on. One day I got a letter from Ian Hamilton saying he'd been watching my work, liked it, and suggesting we meet. I was so unaware of the ways of the literary world that I had no idea I'd been forwarding poems Ian had returned from the *Review* to the same man at the *TLS*.

The notion of mentoring wasn't current then, but Ian was a significant figure in my life: first as someone who promoted my work, but also as a friend. There were no 'mentoring sessions'; he simply gave me the occasional – usually crucial – note: 'This poem ends two lines earlier than you think... are you sure you want this word?... is this really what you mean?...' And he was unfailingly accurate. Ian could go to the heart of a poem and find its flaws at a glance.

Of all the responses I got from him, I think most of two. The first when he took 'Dreams of the Dead' – a long poem – for the *New Review*: 'I don't fully understand it, but I know it's an important poem.' Having said that, he went on to suggest breaking the sections with fictitious dates, which reshaped the poem and made more sense of it. The second, after reading *News from the Front*: 'It's a terrific book, but your way of making a poem hasn't changed; you need to move on.' I asked him if he had any notion of what 'move on' might mean, but he shrugged as if to say, who knows? We were having lunch at the time: an event in Ian's life that invariably involved much smoking and little eating. The conversation went this way and that. When we were leaving the restaurant, as an afterthought, he said 'Oh, I don't know. Try lengthening your line.' The result was *A Bird's Idea of Flight*. I think that in suggesting I break the predominant (though not invariable) line-patterning of earlier books, he was hoping for a tonal change. And that happened. I'm not sure that line-length, in the end, had much to do with it, but he prompted the notion of a need for some compositional change and tone that became part of that. I might add that *News from the Front* was pivotal in other ways, not least in that it was the last, and I think the best, of those largely fictional 'experience-based' collections. Perhaps Ian was ahead of me in seeing that.

P McC: A lot of people nowadays seem to think the best way of becoming a 'published' poet is to do a Creative Writing degree (though I know you are, or have been, Professor of Creative Writing at the University of Roehampton), and/or to win numerous prizes in almost unheard-of competitions. How do you view this? I don't think a gift like yours can be taught.

DH: You can't teach gift, but you can nurture it. You can't supply vision, but you can encourage eyes to open.

P McC: How did you actually teach Creative Writing? Did you have a special method, recipe?

DH: See above. It's a matter of helping the writer identify what's good while being pitiless in pointing out what's poor. The poetry is in the pitiless.

P McC: Did your writing of crime novels (presumably to earn a living?) help to cudgel your poetic skills? Was there a crossover between the two genres?

DH: Yes, to earn a living. I reached a point where I'd had more than enough of publishing – a ten-year panic-attack, really – and had myself fired in a way that proved financially…useful. I turned to writing thrillers because I'd spent ten years editing popular fiction, thrillers included, and I thought I could knock out some dark, violent, bloody, obsessive prose. It would take me about three months to write a hundred-thousand words (standard thriller extent) and, though the money came in stages that gave me enough to live on.

Al Alvarez was a fan of my thrillers. There must have been some crossover between crime fiction and poetry, because Al maintained that the writing – style, word-choice, most of all image – would have enabled him to see through my pseudonyms had he not been in the know. Others have found similar comparisons: in narrative, in compositional choices. I can sort of see it, but didn't know I was doing it. I used to inscribe the books to Al: *Same brain, different name.*

P McC: Your association with Agenda *has been a long one and poems of yours published in its pages through the decades. When did you first appear in* Agenda*? In the era of William Cookson and Peter Dale? Then, more so than now, to have one's poetry published in highly-regarded journals helped to get the attention of respected publishers. Now it all seems to be kudos from competitions, social networking via the media, and millions of tiny presses springing up from almost nowhere, don't you agree?*

DH: I can't be accurate about the first poem in *Agenda* or remember what it was. Definitely when William was running the show, yes.

There's always a fair amount of bad poetry being written. The internet free-for-all does seem to have enabled the eager talentless; but there's good work to be found online. The recent proliferation of small presses and poetry comps…well…it's a skirmish, but I don't think it matters much. In the end, the good is no less evident than the bad.

P McC: You have deservedly won every major poetry prize, it seems to me, including the international Griffin Prize. Has this changed you or your poetry at all? I know Seamus Heaney said that getting the Nobel Prize really ruined his poetry. I suppose he couldn't live a normal private life hidden away in Co Wicklow any more, with so many duties and expectations laid on him. Is it the same with you?

DH: Did Seamus say that – ruined? He published fine poems after 1995. I can see it might have caused a block… maybe that's what he meant. He wrote to me saying that my Ritsos versions – *In Secret* – 'brought me alive again after a dormant spell', but this was some years after he got the Nobel, so no connection between that dormancy and Swedish gong. I know the call on him, as with other Nobel laureates I expect, was severely interruptive, so the contemplative time needed for composition would have been adversely affected. He must have meant that.

I can't remember ever having had a significant lay-off. By the time a collection is being launched, I'm usually well into the next one. I think that's far from unique. Just at the moment, I'm writing every day and have a pretty full publication programme up to 2024.

Prizes are nice to get: readership goes up, and the money certainly helps. On two occasions prizes have saved me from financial meltdown. In the end, though, the work is what it is and will be assessed regardless of gongs and honours. Sometimes the best get missed. Think of Geoffrey Hill.

P McC: Indeed. Your astounding collections have appeared from Faber with regularity over the years…. You never seem to run out of inspiration, for example, your ambitious new collection, Loss, *which we will discuss later.*

DH: Whatever it is that I don't run out of is a mystery to me. Lines arrive…I develop them… it's all opportunity and happenstance…

P McC: What actually inspires you to write, especially sequences? I notice you often make up your own myths such as that memorable long poem, or sequence, I published of yours in the 'Poetry and Opera' issue of Agenda, *'The Salt Wife'. It hovers delicately between dream and reality, between this world and another, almost surreal world at times in its sensuousness. Is the Salt-Wife an ideal woman, your anima, or muse?*

DH: Well, sequences are a means to narrative. I don't plan for that – writing thematically, I mean; rather a story develops or characters take hold. 'The Salt Wife' was originally written to be set to music: and that might still happen. I'd written about the selkie before, and for a composer; obviously I wasn't done with that wild betrayer, nor with her link to music.

Roger Garfitt once made mention of 'the feral woman' in my work. I think she crops up in various guises. The Garden Goddess, for example, who appears – returns – from time to time, the women in *Dreams of the Dead*, the woman who haunts poems like 'Elsewhere' *(Night)* and 'A Dream Book' *(Fire Songs)*, and so on. My forthcoming collection (2024) is a series of sequences, some of which involve complex, oblique, relationships. I've just completed a twelve-poem sequence about angels. Someone who has read the sequence asked me why all the angels are women. Angels are feral, wouldn't you say?

P McC: You said in your essay 'Words for Music' ('Poetry and Opera' issue of Agenda*), 'I am essentially a narrative poet who trades off of a lyrical vocabulary'. Do you feel it is the narrative that gives the poem or sequence its drive? And how important do you think narrative is in today's poetry?*

DH: Harrison Birtwistle was once asked what he thought he'd brought to contemporary music: what difference he'd made. With a deceptive simplicity, he said, 'I tried to do something with pulse.' I would say I tried to do something with the lyric. Even when I was part of the (often misdescribed) group of which Ian Hamilton was the centre (the short love-lyric said to be typical of the group's output), I was finding ways of extending lyrical encounters to narrative sequences, was looking for a complex narrative continuum, something that had the range, the emotional heft and depth of character, that would involve the reader as might a novel, though the story would be episodic (a necklace of short poems) and so revelatory in a piecemeal sort of way. I think that, in my childhood, I took the border ballads to be a sort of verse novel: the protagonists of 'Tam Lin' were also those of 'The Demon Lover' and 'Matty Groves'. 'The Twa Corbies' were ever present. 'Westron Wynde' – another touchstone poem that did then, does now, and will always, prickle the hairs of my head – was part of the drama. There's a novel in that charged quatrain.

So, as I've said, writing sequentially – thematically – is to do with my instinct for narrative. It's important to me and was from the outset. Peter Porter made the point in an early review, noting my 'commitment to lyricism' and going on to say that my method for not 'isolating the shining moment' was 'the dramatic sequence'. But not everything I write is part of a sequence' Think of *Elsewhere*, think of *Sang the Rat*, think of *Rota Fortunae*, and so on. Not only that, some of my sequences don't look for a developed narrative: they're more to do with subject than story: the four 'Fire Songs', for example, don't tell a story, though they do have a unifying image and a central character as a narrative device.

P McC: It is interesting how you diversify, for example, in writing libretti for various operas, and how you articulate the complexity of this in the 'Words for Music' essay. You say 'The way I approach the task is to write, in manuscript, what might be taken for a stage play' – do you approach your own poetry, not linked to opera, in the same way?

DH: No. When I'm writing libretti, I'm very aware of the fact that the words will be uttered and will, for the most part, carry the narrative. So I do set out to write something much like a play. It might be fragmentary or radical in terms of narrative progression but it will depend, primarily, on character, event, action and response. It would be possible to have an opera – and I like the idea enormously – in which almost nothing happens, but no one has asked me for that yet. One of the reasons for my involvement with the opera stage is that word: *stage*. If obliged to choose, I would most often take theatre over screen. Something to do with the contract between stage and auditorium, between actors and audience; something to do with the tensions of live performance; to do with space and the way space is occupied. The specificities of stage are simply not those of screen, which is not, in any way, to denigrate the latter. I spent a long time writing for TV and have written things for screen that would – of course – have been lost on stage. I wish I'd had more opportunity to write for screen: close-up and close-focus provide opportunities for narrative direction and narrative flow that stage, by its nature, can't offer. I remember that Beckett once said – having seen and hated a television performance of *Godot* – that a perfect subject for screen would be, simply, a woman knitting. 'You could go from her hands to her face,' he said, 'then back to her hands, then…' It must have seemed trivial to those disappointed by his response to TV-*Godot*, and I dare say he was being gently sardonic, but it's actually a pretty accurate observation. I can see that visual exchange as a leitmotiv background gesture: a sort of emotional reference to developing narrative events. I could write it.

P McC: I suppose writing libretti is even more complicated than translating a poem from or into a different language, with a lot of give and take and compromise involved… You have the original music of the poem (you so rightly say, 'If I can't hear the music, it's not a poem), the music of the orchestra that divides into the music written by the composer and of the individual instruments and their players – many different voices that all have to connect...

DH: The only compromise, really, is the librettist's and that's as it should be: well, not so much a compromise as part of the deal. Before the composer starts to set the libretto, you have a piece of writing composed according to rules set up by the librettist. Once that piece of writing is set to music, you have something quite different: you have the opera. Librettists who complain that their words can't be understood, or their lines have been broken and reshaped, are missing the point. At the première of *Gawain*, I was sitting next to Michael Tippett. At the end of the first act, when Liz Laurence and Marie Angel had been singing the turning of the seasons from a blue neon hoop just under the flies for some twenty-five minutes, he leaned towards me and said, 'You can never understand the sopranos, Darling.' My response was to seek out Jeremy Isaacs and ask for sur-titles.

P McC: And now for translation itself. Your recent little pamphlet from Rack Press, comprising the Resistance sequence, Homeland, Eighteen Bitter Songs, *Versions of Yannis Ritsos (whom you translated before in* In Secret), *links subtly to your musings on the dichotomy between poetry and song, and so back to opera. We are told in the Introduction that Ritsos thought he had written songs, not poems, to accompany Theodorakis' popular musical setting. But now, in the introduction, John Kittmer says 'These are not artless lyrics of the sort that popular tune-makers were using in those years'... This is exactly it: your libretti are rare jewels, like Ritsos' Homeland; neither of you are mere 'tune-makers'.*

DH: I spent most of the first lockdown – though I'd begun earlier – making versions of the poems Yannis Ritsos wrote when he was in a prison camp on Leros and, after that, under house arrest on Samos. This was during the Papadopoulos junta of the late 'sixties and early 'seventies. Bloodaxe will publish the full collection, *A Broken Man in Flower*, in 2023. Theodorakis – himself in prison -- somehow managed to get a message to Ritsos asking for short pieces he could set to mirror the miseries and brutalities being suffered by the Greek people. Theodorakis had, of course, set Ritsos's long poem 'Epitaphios' which made Ritsos famous; the Metaxas regime publicly burned the book in front of the Acropolis. *The Bitter Songs* consist of eighteen double couplets: an outpouring of sorrow and outrage and defiance. Their music, like mine, in these versions and in my own work, is that of verse composition: notation of a different measure.

P McC: How difficult was it to revivify these compressed song-poems? Each one seems to sing hauntingly into the white paper space around it. Do you know Greece well, and Greek?

DH: Thanks to my appalling education, I am monolingual. I work by triangulating more or less literal versions of the poems. Many poets who make versions do this. The argument between those who insist on a word-for-word representation of the original and those who bring the poem into (say) English in what they take to be a way truer to the poem, has long since petered out into irrelevance, though anyone who wants the last word on it should read Don Paterson's *Appendix: Fourteen Notes to the Version* in his versions of Rilke's *Sonnets to Orpheus*.

P McC: Interesting that Ritsos originally wrote Homeland *in one day and revised it two years later. You too told me you translated/did versions of these Songs in a compressed time, during Lockdown.*

DH: Ritsos was both fast and prolific. Given that the *Bitter Songs* make only seventy-four lines in all, Lockdown (why does it seem that word requires an initial capital?) was more than enough time for versions of them and of many more. Throughout I had the help of John Kittmer, a Ritsos scholar and, at one time, our ambassador to Greece: most often I needed his advice on matters of interpretation, though sometimes, I would ask, 'What did he mean by this' and John would reply, 'Your guess is as good as mine.'

P McC: I love the end line of 'The People': 'Stones will shatter when they sing that song'. This could well apply to both you and to Ritsos when you sing your songs. Also relevant to you both is that wonderful image of the You in the poem 'The Song' being fixed on the bird – 'Soon you will sing the song it has forgotten'.

DH: I tried that line several different ways before it came right…seemed to me to come right.

P McC: And now on to the recent full collection of yours, Loss *(Faber & Faber, 2020). This strikes me as being a vital apocalyptic poem of our time, highly sophisticated in content and structure, and demanding on the reader. As John Burnside affirms: you are 'a master of the human drama'. This – shall I say – complex long poem could be studied forever, so many fluent strands, images and depths to tease out as a whole cosmos is intricately invoked. Were you aware of all these in the composing of it?*

DH: It started as a linkage of jottings and groups of lines in my notebook and on the computer, that I labelled 'Red Mist'. My poems – sequences – narratives – often open up as a series of images around which lines gather and progress before I have any real notion of meaning and direction. With *Loss,* the lines just insisted until I could more or less see what was going on. That probably sounds unlikely, or over-inked, too much of the poetic afflatus, but it's what happened. I got hold of that sonnet / short lines / quatrain structure pretty quickly, but I wasn't at all sure of why it seemed to work. After I'd written a few sections, the images and compositional tendencies became part of the patterning. I'd found the form, in other words, or it had found me.

In my more recent work, I have been glad to allow repetition when it offered itself: repeated images, words, sometimes lines: I consider them touchstones. They fall into place in the same way as (I assume) musical repetition does for composers and visual repetition for painters. A reader might go back through my work to find the ways in which those images, words, lines have brought pressure and music of a different sort to this passage of work or that; and, when taken together, they would form a sort of force-field over disparate lines, sequences, even books. A less investigative approach will find repetition, anyway, in individual sequences, and certainly in my next collection. As I say: touchstones.

P McC: Loss is so clever in its patterning and structure, repetition used as part of the overall pattern; it reads so very fluently that at times it almost seems like subconscious or automatic writing, yet it is very controlled in its diversity…

DH: I guess I took this remark into my last answer.

P McC: To me there are echoes of Beckett, the main character, the 'he' or the 'you' a kind of everyman alone in the universe with his repeated cry of angst, 'salve me' as he faces the void, and houses, rooms, doors, faces 'that paper your walls', a time 'that shunts and stalls' and words that 'unspeak', with silence always lurking.

DH: I wouldn't want to unpick or interrogate those lines and images, but you're right to make mention of them in terms of the book's structure and direction.

P McC: It is, in general, a savage indictment of the age we live in, all of us with our 'willing blindness', (which seems to link to Gurdjieff's notion how most of us live not fully conscious in a 'waking sleep' and this view was also enlarged upon in Eliot's Four Quartets*),'the worst already with us/ dogfight politics barrel-bombs/ children scorched faceless/ deluge and wildfire'…*

DH: I have come to draw more and more on the conflict and outrage of current politics (or that provoked by current politics), though not in any direct, agitprop manner. The four 'Fire Songs' that formed the backbone of the book of that name all came from a deep concern about the climate crisis, not least among them the (by some) grotesquely misinterpreted 'A Song for Mistress Askew'.

I don't see how these overwhelming matters of life and death that press on us daily can be avoided: the end of any structured global civilisation; the heat-death of the planet…

P McC: You cover the theme of loss in so many ways, some more obvious such as the loss of ego, existential loss of meaning, loss of life, of memory, loss of love, of trinkets – and some more subtle losses. For example, in the syntax throughout there is little or no punctuation which, if punctuation is logic, could imply the loss of logic or of meaning, with the reader having actively to find a sense in order to interpret what is being said. The long columns of poetry in the main parts of each section line up like thick prison bars, implying loss, even, of freedom and what is left is often at a remove in stage-sets and 'curtain calls'. Did you intend all this or does this demonstrate poetry's elasticity of meaning?

DH: Oh, the latter, for sure. But I'm intrigued by your interpretation, not least the prison bars image. If by 'curtain calls' you're referring to the quatrains at the end of each section, that's a very apt description. I'll probably hijack it.

The scant punctuation offered itself as a means of propulsion: something less measured. I didn't see it coming: I began to notice it, then encouraged it. Colons became the punctuation of choice.

I didn't intend any of the patterning you mention, at least not from the outset; it evolved. You see something you like and start to develop it. In the case of *Loss*, some of those things worked for the entire sequence and helped make it; in others it was more local.

P McC: At times you use religious imagery with Christ, the crucifix, the agony in the garden, prayers, angels whether fallen or not – do you mean these as some kind of reprieve from the nihilism of everything else, even if it is all a 'dumb-show' with 'the shadow-play of sin and redemption'? Even the 'white' that is threaded through this work becomes a 'thin-white near-black' at the end, and it could be said that neither white nor black are primary colours, white signifying a blank, an ultimate white-out, and black an end, death, a black-out, contributing to the overall nothingness of existence.

DH: I was brought up a Baptist: or, rather, my aunt was 'saved' by Billy Graham and felt I should be saved, too. Baptists are a pretty fervent lot. I quickly learned that the louder you sing the more certain you are of salvation. The sermons were classic nonconformist fire and brimstone. In retrospect, I think I must have liked all that, or discovered some sort of affiliation to it, even found it necessary, perhaps. Certain lines from certain hymns are locked in my brain. This, for example, which I made use of in *News from the Front:* 'We will never doubt Thee, though Thou hid'st Thy Light / Life is dark without Thee, death with Thee is bright.' That salted itself away when I was about ten years old. Fiona Sampson, in a review of (I think) *Night*, suggested that the rhythms of the Baptist Hymnal are as evident in my work as those of the Border Ballads. I know the Bible pretty well. The Easter story was electrifying to me; in a way, it still is. So those images, those references, are part of my stock-in-trade.

To be clear, I'm not a Christian, though when asked that question once, I replied, 'No, but I would want to make a case for Christ'. Not long since, I wrote the libretto for an oratorio (music by Sally Beamish) called *The Judas Passion*. It told the Easter story with Judas Iscariot as the protagonist. Judas wasn't quite my invisible friend when I was a child, but he certainly put in an appearance from time to time. Of all the reading in and around the subject that I did, what affected me most concerned the fact that Judas was abandoned during the harrowing of hell. Writing of this, the theologian Anthony Cane said that if Judas's remorse was unacceptable to God, then there was an incoherence in the economy of salvation. I worked the piece up from that notion, and from my understanding that, in the moment when Judas left the cenacle (*Judas went out and it was night*, to slightly paraphrase John 13:30), Christendom began. Writing the oratorio with those things in the forefront of my mind, brought home to me that Christian imagery and scripture are part of the way I see the world. That's a very circumlocutory way of saying that images, or examples, in my work of the sort you mention are usually what they seem.

In answer to the last part of your question, in a black/white dichotomy I think of black as erasure, so something, I suppose, that might be restored or rediscovered. White is death: effacement: end of everything. Utter loss.

P McC: *Recently, David, I was sent from Guillemot Press an exquisitely beautiful hard-back book,* Salt Moon, *in which you collaborate with your very gifted, prize-winning photographer son, Simon. This book, that you told me was a 'before I die' book, is a real treasure, even physically to hold and to turn its quality-paper pages. It is a tremendous double-act: father and son, the black and white photographs with their intense textures of the sea's elemental mystery under the light of the salt moon, and the sacred, sparse, lyrical poems showing 'patterns of light/ opening/ versions of themselves'. The poems enhance the photographs and the photographs enhance the poems... Can you tell us more about this special collaboration, a first, I think, for you two?*

DH: Simon is a significant artist; his vision is compelling. He took those photographs of moonlight striking the sea some time ago – maybe a decade. Over the years I had gone back to them again and again, but never felt moved to write. In fact, when he asked me to suggest a title, I gave him *Salt Moon* long before *Salt* or *The Salt Wife* had come to mind. I was looking – or had been looking – at them when two images presented themselves: tideline detritus and a black Madonna. And soon after that, the notion of a bird that makes landfall to 'roost in its own stain'. And I was off. The photos are hypnotic and endlessly subtle.

You say it's a beautiful book and so it is, thanks to Luke Thompson at Guillemot Press. In fact, Simon and I have worked together before: three poster poems for an Australian World Wildlife conservationist campaign, and for an extraordinary series of photos he took of a woman underwater (can't be described: have to be seen) one of which, plus a commissioned poem, was featured by the Sydney Opera House. Those collaborations were important to me, but once I'd started to write the *Salt Moon* poems a full-length book became a 'before I die' project.

P McC: This Salt Moon *that you have just accomplished with your son could almost be a special kind of Coda to* Loss: *there is a house, rooms, window panes, black and white, repeated images knitting the poems together. Yet here, despite the black Madonna and the sea's junk, the lyrical prevails with the sea in all its different lights, glints, vastness and swells:*

the frenzy of shoreline stones
in the draw of the tides; take one: its heart
is that frantic pulse in your palm...

DH: Repetitions, yes: images; the liminal aspects of windows and doors: also what they reveal and conceal, birds in flight, water, lyric progression… It's all one.

P McC: Now, David, can you tell us about your next collection, a few poems of which we are glad to print here? Your output is extraordinary as you produce collections which all differ from one another, are all class acts.

DH: I'll just say that it's a series of sequences; they trade off each other while retaining their own integrity. They differ in subject, but a thread of repetition integrates them tonally. A couple of the sequences will appear, whole, or in part, as tasters before publication: one, from Fine Press Poetry, comes this year; another, later, from Dare-Gale Press, after that another from Guillemot. Sort of calling cards for the new collection: which will, I think, be a fairly long book. And I'm glad that some are in this issue to, in a small way, inform this interview.

P McC: Do you see the whole corpus of your work as one long passionate continuum? Towards the end of Loss, *it seems that your own voice intervenes, like some contemporary film director, to define what is going on, even if, as usual throughout the sequence, nothing is what seems:*

This is the draft of a scene from a drama called 'Loss'.
Stage directions call for gestures of distress.
White stalks white, soft-footed, murderous.

And the final rhetorical question: 'Why not/ give in to heartbreak?' as, let us all hope, you continue 'to live' with 'this press of words'.

DH: I think that, increasingly, my collections might be read one in the light of another, which doesn't mean that they're in any way interdependent: as critics have observed, as you observe, my books are very unlike one another in terms of form and subject. Think of the difference between *A Bird's Idea of Flight* and *Night*, between *Fire Songs* and *Salt*, between each of those books and *Loss*. I never (I know some poets do) sit down with a given task: now a book on this subject; now a book on that. I'm not suggesting there's something wrong with that; in fact, having a plan, a specific subject, strikes me as a likeable notion. But I never really have any idea of what's coming beyond the poem in hand as it takes shape: I simply follow the lead on which my compositional instinct insists.

Hilary Davies

O Magnum Mysterium

Time, that is, grace and circumstance
Acting on our good will.
Circumstances handed me this sentence.
In the lee of a hill
I took it and went to sit
At the edge of a wood
With my back to a tree.
There was a scent of wet and wild garlic
But the wood behind me
Was still of wind and birds.
Deep to deepening still.

How do we reach into silence?
You cannot touch it, nor hold it, nor pour it.
You cannot describe it, nor say what it is.
Words snuff out silence.
That's when it most eludes.
Ah, but to believe by that
It is a thing of nothing
Is to mistake imperception
For absence.
Water, being formless
And tasteless and colourless,
For all that moves mountains.

Makers of music know this:
Chords spring out of the span of silence
Not from empty space
Across which a rat may scuttle.
The drummer in equipoise,
His arms silent,
Upturned to the air;
The conductor also,
Holding his structures
On the tip of a wand.

In silence forces reveal themselves
Like creatures who fly only at dusk,
Far more intimate to us
Than we can ever be.

This was the circumstance.
Here at the rough bole of the tree
Upright on the hillside:
Deeper and deeper into its branches
The onrush of the sky,
Heaven's blue dowry.

The leaves listened.
Not a sigh.

Then the tree opened
And I saw through the bark
Living fire in channels
Going up and down;
The tree was a flowing column:
Green, amber, gold
Plunging and rising;
Salamanders and dragonflies
Played at its core.
Out of its branches deltas of light
Spread over the green ground.
And yet the trunk stood taut and still
Even as its body teemed.
Earth's hearth and air's fall
Bounded in the grace of time
In the tree.

So it may be when a woman sits
In a room alone
Her thoughts open by the lily-blown window
And, on a sudden, feels
The downdraught of heaven within her.

Elizabeth Barton

The Linnet

My mother is searching for a word.
It flits through the hedgerow of her thought,

flutters in her throat, but the word won't come.
Almost forty years ago, a stroke stole her song.

Wire by iron wire, she tore the cage
of her isolation down, reclaimed two languages.

She makes up for the gaps with gesture,
expression, her face a ripening field of wheat,

her fingers quivering like linnet's wings.
There's a game we play to keep the rhythm flowing –

she tells a story; I know it so well, I sense the words
she'll stumble over, fill the silences. It's the nouns

that elude her – she's trying to translate the name
of her grandparents' farm across the marsh, Dôlawel.

She closes her eyes, puts three fingers to her brow,
touches her lips, as though she's willing brain

and tongue to work in harmony, as though this rite
could coax the words from the thistles of her mind.

She pictures herself riding home through fields
of buttercups, tastes the sea's salt breath

and the words take flight.

Note: Dôlawel: Welsh for *Meadow Breeze*

Inheritance

It hangs on the landing, a photo of my mother
riding side-saddle on a chestnut mare
to celebrate the Coronation.

She's just sixteen, leading the parade
along Dundonald Avenue, hailed
by hills and sheep. She carries no whip,

holds the reins one-handed.
She thought they'd pick an English girl
to be the Queen, not her, a farmer's daughter,

riding wild through Rhuddlan Marsh.
She looks more bird than soldier,
like a goldfinch poised for flight,

white-plumed, black-capped, dazzle of gold
and scarlet. I cannot see myself in her
but I can see my daughter –

they share the same dark hair, a warmth,
a fearlessness. My mother is smiling
but the photo's been hand-coloured,

giving her an otherworldly sheen,
her face ghost-pale, her tunic too red-raw,
reminding me of the courage of a girl

who came so close to death
and I can almost touch the wound
a mother passes to her daughter.

Matthew Barton

Singing Lessons

The more I tried to loosen
my tongue, to root
my breath to its spring
in the pelvic ground,
the more I seized up: distress
at breath constricted, song
sticking in my throat; at this
knot I am and all its disconnect.

But today I woke at dawn
not into time and space but to
that blackbird's utter flute,
its sputter of clicks, its spendthrift fling
and swanee whistle plunge
and then

a silence even lovelier: for now
I heard it listening intent
to all the stillness it had made
come rushing back from far-flung hills and fields -

like trusting when you give yourself away
entirely life comes pouring back.

Kate Ashton

Mother Tongue

It's not that the gate was left open
but what has passed through –
tides of lapis lazuli
jade sways of sea
and spring after spring the doe that bows
beneath lichened ash bough the colour
of her hide

we always knew new life would come
of it until last year's
full flower moon
hung luscious as
ripe apricot   a blush that shrank from touch
filled mouths with Tantalean watering
and outright shame

at first they came with babes in arms
sweet suckling sons and
daughters drenched in
desert dust and
oud and shimmering they came   eyes kohled
and turned aside from rude insolence
and flagrant lies

what overcame us then was ancient:
they crept ashore bowed low
before us on
bare knees like old
wisdom open at the page we'd closed   the day
we lost our sight of things to come
as was foretold

some said it was nothing but old news
no truth but rumour
feeling its way
like fate or some
lost traveller apostate   mired in myth
apocrypha afloat on unclean air
like vagrant motes

we felt the darkling spin of space move in
to steal our breath away
lostness beyond
hope like letting
go of some safe hold   on worlds beyond
ravenous reach of entropy and grief
some certain home

they spoke old tongues we did not know
held fast to their beliefs
knelt to the stone
that holy place
with hands open in prayer   the way
they read the Book of Truth
of everywhere

we looked into their eyes to find ourselves
unclothed as dethroned deities
aloof itinerants
who faced iconoclasm
at the gate   because we'd lost
the words for womb for welcome
and good faith

Annemarie Ní Churreáin

A Public Address by The New Republic

When the blood comes, you must be quiet and still.
To become a woman is to become not unlike an animal.
Underneath a pillow you will find a book tonight.
A virgin is a girl who has, or has not yet, worn a veil.
A sinner is a girl who plays a game with herself.
Whatever you do, do not fall into the company of a slut.
Whatever you do, do not forget you have a mother.
Nobody wants to walk in a garden where the ivy is torn.
Nobody wants a daughter who lies down in the muck.
When you lie down with a man you may at first feel ill.
When a child is born, it is born out of the pit.
When a child is born a priest must clean and bless the mother's bones.
A mother is a woman who nurses her child in the dark.
If a child is born to another child we must stay behind the curtain.
If a child is born without a father everyone will know.
The dictionary is a catalogue of filthy words.
Another name for the female body is *lord have mercy*.
If you say a prayer backwards in the mirror you will make the Virgin weep.
If you turn your calculus upside down you will go to hell. Mary
Magdalene was a whore until she was forgiven.

I Dream of My Sister's Agony

Did it begin with a whisper?

A prayer into the ear so perfectly composed of
whorls & star-bones
& god-willing.

I dream of my sister's agony
the sound is first

a seed,
a wing thumping against a pane,
wheels whirring like rubber moons

and then a string of syllables
like wells spilling over *my*
child, my child.

The New Republic says: *offer it up*.
The New Republic disapproves *please, why, what if?*
The New Republic consists of falling.
Like dead ravens.
Like blades of rain. Like sickles of light diminishing.

Timothy Houghton

Gold-Cornered Square

old-fashioned photo corners

On the next black page
of an album half empty,
my aunt left a gold-cornered square.
Black-and-white faces
fill early pages. For whom
is this square waiting? God maybe. Gold
would be debased
by current times: colour pics diminish
gravity. In the garden,
shaded wingstem protects many birds
who don't show themselves
for even a glimpse.
I will keep the gold square black
and open a new album,
and fill plastic sleeves.
After all, mom loved colour, animals,
the Fauvist blast. This could work.
It takes effort to avoid the dark parties
in any risen
abyss. Thoughts of mom last too long
too many mornings. Pursuing sleep,
I sometimes hear the phone ring
when it does not ring.
I'm primed and ready
for the next emergency. In a dream,
the gold square waits with God
and waits for her
in the album of black pages.

Merryn MacCarthy

The Long Road

Another Spring just beginning
and soon a new confinement.
A blackbird on my lawn doesn't sing.

To gather my forces I head South,
our route of old to holidays
in the magical Pyrenées.

But the hospital where I lost you
looms, the road a piercing arrow
ready to be released.

The long road to the mountains
is Roman. I need ways
more Celtic, winding.

A familiar hamlet tucked into foothills
draws me, the sound of water healing.
All is hazy, a mere illusion

of high, snow-capped peaks.
I detour upwards cautiously, woods
bursting with young leaf, birdsong,

and suddenly, unaccountably
you drift across smiling
from within the trees.

For me of lost belief
I will now forever see you
rising, rising out of my grief.

Easter

Then he died
and the distance
is too great.
Under the cypresses
I can't find him.

Is he at peace
in this burial place?
The cut-back wisteria
blooms as never before,
heavy with grief.

Arum lilies, iris spears,
lilacs torment me.
It is Summer too soon
after a Spring
he didn't see.

There is no rock
to roll back,
only plants to tend
where he wished to be laid
in the earth's folded furrow.

Caroline Maldonado

Other dimensions

(Michelangelo)

He chooses stone to subtract from.
Words, he adds.
One to another.
Sometimes a word
calls to marble dust
on the line below with a song
and a surface warmed by sun.

From space he creates halls and high ceilings.
He understands dimensions
knows the walls of his home are limited
as the streets leading to his workshop
as Italy's warring states
as the weight of his own life.
He believes the world
is limited.

From marble he carves an angel, a mother
or son that touches the heart
and reveals a soul but words
can travel though time, travel through space
sending love to la Marchesa in Rome.
In this way a small poem
may grow larger than David
or even St Peter's Basilica.

There's stone and the pigments
he grinds to create a paradise
and hell with him in it
and there are poems chiselled in pain
yet still neither word nor stone
is enough for him. What I seek
he writes to her again
is heaven alone.

Stone 1

It's by
taking away
that one draws from the stone
a live figure. It grows greater
in stone.

Much as
the excess that
is one's own flesh with its
coarse skin may hide some good works in
the soul.

Mirror

In his room, a mirror though not for vanity.
His works unfinished. The body beautiful
as a semi-carved angel. Scraps pinned
to walls, sketches of young madonnas,
building designs, a pencilled figure
bent back, a bow facing that chapel's
half-painted dome. Drawings on one
side of the paper, poems on the other.
Ink bleeds through. Already beyond
himself, when they cut off his boots

the leather came away with his soles' flesh.

Stone 2

He will not sit, the old man.
His time is brief. It's not like slicing
skin from a fruit to taste the sweet flesh inside,

the flesh itself he must chisel away
until that other man, the one the block
held before, the one embracing the fallen Redeemer

becomes the grieving mother.
You can see the shadow of his face still imprinted on her veil,
that dark shape is the hollow of his eye.

The sculptor, shoeless, his crumbling spine aflame
strips flesh from limb
hollows the torso.

Only by taking away *per forza di levar*
can he release the spirit
and so he carves,

hammers, the sharp of his scarpello
roughing the stone until the figure is ready to slip
into the cavity of the tomb.

Martin Caseley

A Singular Voice Raised in Gratitude

John F. Deane: *Naming of the Bones* (Carcanet, 2021)

This latest substantial collection from John F. Deane returns to a number of themes familiar from his previous volumes: Achill, family, rural Ireland, childhood, music, sacramental landscapes – all are present and correct. Deane's exploring in this volume, however, ploughs deeper and ranges wider, discovering new resonances in some familiar locations. *Naming of the Bones* also includes two ambitious sequences based on the music of Olivier Messiaen and a number of poems with Mediterranean settings.

These Mediterranean poems reveal that wherever he goes, Deane discovers traces of the numinous – hints in the margins of history, as he would put it – revealing kindred or recurring patterns, not all beneficent. Icarus, in the eponymous poem, is described as a 'young man of the Cretan uplands'; as he ascends, he sees his Greek island, the earth revolving through calendrical time 'like a vineyard fruiting and dying back', not unlike an Irish smallholding in the West, then finally plummeting 'over the utmost horizons of our history'. 'The Humming Top', a poem nominally about childhood, also comes to rest with an image of global history:

> knowing already
> how the great world turns and spins...

The child, falling asleep, notices how the natural world depicted on the top blurs, 'the colours fuse', but history remains alive and charged, as 'the humming goes on and on'. For Deane, this charge, running through his memories and the natural world he describes, can be spoken of simply as the indwelling of the Holy Ghost. Writing of the importance to him of Hopkins' 'God's Grandeur', he has written of 'an electricity, that springs forth in praise of that Creator'.[1] In 'I Am', a communion-poem, he further lays out his credentials: 'Jewish-Christian, Hellenist, I am Greco-Roman, Byzantine', allied to 'the original mandate of the Alpha, the Omega Christ'. A 'guest' in the Upper Room, invited to the feast, despite 'full two millennia of a difficult history', he is grateful for the sufficiency of his belief. The

---

[1] *Give Dust a Tongue: A Faith and Poetry Memoir*, John F.Deane, The Columba Press, Dublin, 2015, p. 208.

title echoes this with the mysteries of the Biblical phrase from Exodus, spoken to Moses, 'I am that I am', a statement of gnomic finality, requiring acceptance rather than questioning, while the overarching patterns of a prophetic Christian theory of historical time are also evident.

As is usual in Deane's writing, a number of poems seek to recognise a sense of religious pilgrimage as seen in the lives of saints and fellow-travellers of the gospel. In his previous volume, *Dear Pilgrims* (2018), this was evident throughout, but there are also glimpses here: for example, in companion-poems, the lives of Saints Aidan and Cuthbert are described. The former inhabited 'the straitened life of islands', an itinerant preacher seen as 'a black flame visible along the causeway', the people of Iona and Lindisfarne humbly accepting 'their daily bread'. Cuthbert, on the other hand, lived a life of 'harshness', solicitous for his flock, but inhabitant of a narrower creed, raising only questions, as the concluding stanza of the poem suggests:

> what of the Christ of banquets, what can you say
> of God's most good creation? And what
> of eros, and the waiting arms of the love-lorn Christ?

These contrasting concerns – harvesting in this world, pointing to the world to come – suggest a wide, catholic inclusivity to Deane's approach. This gyre widens still further when, in 'Triple H', the names illuminated include his three poetic fathers Herbert, Hopkins and Heaney. Deane claims these forerunners as equally blessed figures, 'writing outside themselves of themselves inside', and several poems here explore the everyday tasks Herbert claimed as blessings. 'Wood' describes the carpentering abilities of Grandfather Ted as a kind of 'devotion', for instance, yet ends with bathetic images of woodworm and mortality. Hopkins looms greater still, 'Kestrel' providing a glittering picture of a 'vigilante... at-hover in the Hopkins-eye', the bird being an 'excess of fire' and 'tumult of the Lord', a sharpened energy within a dangerous island terrain – a reminder that this poet often writes from within a rugged and unforgiving island territory, whether geographical or historical.

The third of these names, Heaney, remains a more secular inspiration for Deane. In his previous collections, poems such as 'Shelf Life' and 'Butcher' inhabit a clear domestic territory indebted to what he calls here 'the frames/ of dailiness' in Heaney's writings. Here, family resemblances remain, with Deane's portraits admitting the sanctity of rural labour in a way familiar from Heaney's blacksmiths and potato diggers. Furthermore, Deane is not above making explicit doffs of the cap to his contemporary: 'Old Bones' finds the lure of the islands calling. 'This is Ireland, holding her wars,/ her poets, her ruins and her rains, and the holy islands', he confesses to himself, admitting that he is 'lost and at home', an echo of Heaney's famous, troubling lines about sacrifice, during The Troubles, in 'The Tollund Man'.

It will be evident by now, then, that there is a considerable amount of self-questioning going on in these poems. Deane rigorously anatomises and scrutinises his own motivations no less than those of his usual monastic and saintly forebears. A poem like 'Found in the Margins: 6th Century' may begin in a picture of dedicated monastic work – in the scriptorium, in the barns – but a stoneworker chiselling a Christlike shape leads on, not to peaceful, daily prayers but worrying questions instead: the eroding power of faith, the smoke of destruction. Rather than the Holy Ghost being evoked, Deane describes a rapacious kestrel, the 'rasping' nature of psalms being sung, and the 'sheer will' necessary for an individual to continue the monastic struggle. This dark night of one soul is the flip side of Herbert's daily, sunlit tasks, the 'unloving depths' of the dark shores all too real, all too beckoning. Individual short poems such as 'Refugee', about the dreadful drowning of a child whose body is washed ashore, do not shy away from the implications of such recurrent patches of darkness.

An awareness of this darkness also pervades the ambitious sequences based on the music of Olivier Messiaen. The shorter of these, 'Quartet for the End of Time', switches between poetry and prose, providing a commentary on the title piece, composed by Messiaen whilst detained in a prisoner-of-war camp in late 1940. The prose sections, highly compressed, echo the melody lines of the piece whilst also insisting on the cyclical nature of such historical experiences: 'the quartet: Nazis. Taliban. Boko Haram. Isis.' Deane links this almost Yeatsian view of the cycles of history with a prophetic passage from the Book Of Revelation, which inspired the composer: 'Gongs and trumpets, the six trumpets of the Apocalypse with their disasters… and the seventh, *tutti*, telling the end.' Music has long functioned in Deane's work as a source of symphonic patterns, but here it becomes the site of something darker. It is still implicated in Christian belief – 'Listen, the music said: I am standing at the door, knocking…' but, despite the sequence ending in a vision of unity and the crucified Christ, the final image is more disturbing:

> we are… one in the gentle taking of hands
> through the long, darkening night.

The prose-poem sections, whilst mostly descriptive, find analogues for various instruments: clarinet, for example, is 'owl-hoot' or blackbird, piano passages are visualised as providing 'chutes of emerald downscales'. In places, however, Deane imposes his own belief-patterns on what he hears: another passage is described as 'Pre-Genesis, post-Apocalypse', something visualised in abstract eternal terms, leading to themes which culminate in 'Christogenesis and notes sounding towards an Amen.' The centrality of Christ's death also permeates several other poems, notably 'No Offence Intended', where the viscerality of the brutal death of 'the outlaw Christ' is juxtaposed with innocent children playing beneath the everyday crucifixions. The laconic tone of the title brings to mind a similar contrast in Auden's 'Musée des Beaux Arts': Deane's use of the quotidian and the cosmic again recalls the twin poles of Herbert and Hopkins.

'Like the Dewfall', the second, longer Messiaen-inspired sequence, takes a slightly different approach, being seven reflections on lives of gratitude, related to 'Visions de l'Amen', a suite of seven pieces for two pianos. The Biblical numerology, it will be seen, remains important, and the entire sequence is structured, like Messiaen's music, on a phrase from the Catholic writer Ernest Hello, celebrating thankful lives lived between the moment of Genesis and the fulfilment of Revelation. Accepting the need to be a prophetic witness in such times, alongside this Biblical timespan, Deane places his own 'Ages of Man', beginning with childhood, working through schooldays, early manhood, married life, being called as a poet, and ending in domesticity and spiritual encounters which hint at the cyclical nature of life – a notion encapsulated in the title image of the daily, endless miracle of dewfall.

In the earlier sections, powerful memories shape the young poet: he learns 'there are stations of sadness/ on the long journey, from *introibo* towards *amen*' and in the local monastery he hears the Messiaen piece played on 'two/ grand pianos, winged and elegant, like seraphim'. The music performed is 'furious/ as thunder-burst' and returning to the monastery graveyard years later, the poet is 'conscious again of our world's grace, aware/ of hurrying time, of who you are, and when, and where', grateful to be granted such an epiphany. The poet journeys through life, vouchsafed glimpses of the numinous, until, 'smitten at last with the Christ', he embraces his calling, able later to recognise 'the agape of rock and marigold, and the eros of a selfless sympathy'.

Gratitude is the central theme here, and Deane is highly adept at finding different facets of life to give praise and be thankful for. Having said this, the overall sense of time passing is clear: in the second section the local monastery, fondly recalled, is in ruins; in the fifth, the townland of Leitrim is empty, grassed-over fields; in the sixth, a baptismal font summons the dead ancestors, 'a moment…out of the incomprehensible/ immensity that is time.' There is much in the whole sequence structured around looking back, but also enacting and celebrating an attitude of thankfulness and praise:

> I have sought a living poetry, written out of spiritual
> in the on-going love affair between self and world,
> to yield a deepening understanding and a widening
>
> tenderness, that will save us from the hell of remorseless
> logic...

These lines, from the sixth section of this sequence, 'Point of Pure Truth', encapsulate many of Deane's aims. He seeks to write 'a poetry/ of soul's integrity and venture', and the final section attempts a consummation of these big themes. The Biblical image of a feast is the final setting for such ruminations: 'even the unproductive sand... will flush, after all, into the joy of the festive song of songs', the poet invited, like George Herbert before him, to a gathering from (in a wonderful phrase) the 'all-sainted, infinite demesnes of God'. The very last poem in the sequence quietly and fittingly dramatises Deane's own 'Amen', an elder now, gradually ascending stairs, cradled by domesticity.

In the memoir referred to earlier, Deane writes of working towards a poetry of faith, encouraged by the words of Denise Levertov and others[2], and having the great examples of Herbert and Hopkins always before him. He describes the experience of learning from the act of crafting his own work: 'I do find the answer in the poems themselves... for they show me what I deeply believe, after, and not before, they are written.' Here, then, is a poetry alight in gratitude, displaying all the familial and cultural traces which have enriched Deane since his childhood in Achill, a luminous tapestry which continues to encircle him, bearing him up through whatever darkness may come.

---

[2] Deane, op.cit, pp. 179-180.

Patricia McCarthy

John Burnside: *Learning to Sleep* (Cape Poetry, 2021)

John Burnside is one of the most formidable poets writing in English today. In this, his latest collection, he shows no sign of a lessening in verbal energy and music in his wonderfully consummated poems, all of which link fluently together here, in one majestic body of a long poem written as if effortlessly as he breathes in and out. Burnside is a chronic insomniac, and said, in the interview I did with him in the Dwelling Places issue of *Agenda*, 'I spend a good deal of time consorting with ghosts and phantoms, but they are very good company, much of the time. Sometimes, I fear, I allow myself to think of them as better company than the living, flesh and blood creatures of the day. Which is wrong, in many ways, but those night folk are wonderfully unpredictable and there's an elegance to them that I can't help but admire'.

Although perhaps at first less immediately accessible than usual, it soon becomes clear that Burnside is deliberately less direct than normal in this collection because he is writing as if from a hypnopampic state, half asleep, half awake, with all the attendant random, unrelated, often surreal images that most of us experience in those strange hours. The recognisable poet is at work here, though, as he nevertheless furthers his exploration of the margins between this world and the other, his perspective always big and visionary, his startlingly accurate images painterly.

As usual, he is surrounded by ghosts, some different from those in earlier collections – those of his own mother, past figures, the dead, Arthur Rimbaud, the Old Masters, unknown spirits – that seem to hover between pagan and Christian images. As I noted in my interview with Burnside, this group of images that recur seem totemic or animistic and form a kind of second skin of his. The old land with its often unnamed 'gods' and the over-riding Greek God of Sleep, Hypnos (invoked as the poet tries to come to terms with his longstanding severe sleep disorder). The following few lines of mixed, interwoven imagery early in the collection concentrate his main themes throughout of language, nature, Christian (Catholic) religion, Greek myth, and point the way to what follows, with subtle lessons he sometimes gives himself, in his overall apprenticeship in sleep.

> If everything you love can disappear
> then anything you choose could bring it back,
> handfuls of dusk and grammar, plucked from the air,
> a Midnight Mass
> of *Tannenhaum* and silver.

Orpheus, so they say, could sing a bird
From nowhere…

The Catholicism in which Burnside was brought up, with 'the minor/ Kyries of saints' days', which is residual in his psyche, along with its vestiges of the pagan, whether he has the 'faith' or not – and the surreal juxtaposition of images, enrich the texture of this collection throughout but are never obtrusive. 'I am learning to mourn/ the saints we will never become:/ snow at the back of my head/ and a garment of suede/ hand-stitched with lice and down/ for the next/ extinction.' Another example: 'I occupy the dative like a fallen/mustardseed'.

The strange mix, here, of orthodox religion with the pagan is demonstrated in the 4-part poem 'On Being Pagan', the heart – which can be many things in the book such as 'a cloister', 'a sinkhole' – can be 'an animal, the totem we forgot// in Bible Class, when everything we knew/ was broadcast back to us// as purple noise'.

Beautifully lyrical images, such as

Small rain pitted the windows, years of dreaming

settled on the glass
like spots of dust,

and still, uncanticled, it filled the room:
wolf in the shadows, mongoose in the light…

Even the barn owl 'plucked lifelike from the air' a single word 'in one fell swoop// and shredded, on the cusp of alleluia'.

This reminds me of John F. Deane's new collection, *Naming of the Bones*, (reviewed here by Martin Caseley) when Deane says 'You are on the verge of prayer,/ conscious again of our world's grace, aware/ of hurrying time, of who you are, and when, and where'. Both poets, from different standpoints, seem to embrace the same vision where our ordinary conception of time is questioned, epiphanies abound, or nearly abound, and the mystery at the heart of things is omnipresent. However where Deane's collection resembles a gentle, thought provoking prayer-book in its implicit, deeply rooted Catholic faith, Burnside's hovers between worlds and faiths and, at times, a dark side is more evident. For example, he is aware of 'the way the heart// resumes its darkest form and hunkers down,/ to feed on any sweetmeat it can find.' Past people, too, both those known and unknown, sometimes give a shudder, for they 'only kept you sweet,/ to gut you now'. This shudder is kept in balance, and mainly lessened by the overall botanical beauty of the poet's vision:

> … the oak-woods
> harbouring those guests our fathers knew
> by name, the meadows
> quickening with clouds of Speckled Wood,
> Dingy Skipper, Large White, Holly Blue.

The proper names of the butterflies reinforce the magic with realism, especially today when the butterfly population is in decline.

It is impossible not to wonder at the strength and originality of Burnside's images, how he seems to pluck them from the very air of each poem, too many to quote. One example: in 'Ode to Hypnos' he imagines

> a troupe of all the souls
> we might have been,
> crossing the seven bridges, one by one,
> like Struwwelpeter dolls, with ink for skin
> and nothing to keep them from hurt
> but the promise of dawn.

In another poem he talks of 'the beauteous martyrs I kept in the attic like lodgers,/ clerics in topcoats and scarves in the heat of the night'. The simile and images of recognisable clothes in these two lines are instantly recognisable to the reader and made memorable, as happens throughout.

Burnside interprets the 'Incarnation' not personally but at a remove, through the Old Masters who 'brought the Sacred Heart/ to light', with a different kind of ghosting, 'Hallowmas/ ghosting the walls' while he remains 'lost in the shortfall of now'. The poet, as always, exudes painterly images: a man 'old before his time'

> …watches, while the city fades from quartz
> to plum, from plum
>
> to cochineal, a restless drift
> through subtleties and shades
>
> he cannot
> capture

and he demonstrates here how the special visionary 'now', just like the perfect art form, can never quite be captured or achieved in the 'headlong and unmasterable now/ that slips away, one pier light at a time'.

In part IV, the last part of this poem, the surreal images persist with 'fishnets/snagged with requiem/ and faded bone' followed by the interesting juxtaposition of the 'The Star of Bethlehem' with 'The Southern Cross' that weaves the pagan back into the Christian imagery. For Egyptians, the Southern Cross was the place where Horus. the Sun God, was crucified, marking winter. To the Aborigines and Maori, and I think to Burnside at times in his work as he crosses borders of different beliefs and systems, it symbolises animist spirits integral to astral beliefs.

As already seen in a few details above, Burnside, without being an overtly political ecologist, glorifies our earth with detailed botanical images sprinkled through this collection that confirm him as an already established master of the lyric to whom nature, with its wildernesses and weeds, is as dear as it is to Gerard Manley Hopkins.

Two major themes of language and light are refracted initially through a child's vision. In the first part of 'Indelible', subtitled 'English Speaking Board, 1968', in which he captures that era of 'working men/ distilled to malt and Capstan Navy Cut', even though,.now, as a mature man 'the place names/ tangle and burr on my tongue, these decades later,// the language no longer mine'. Yet he recalls in detail how

> ...they taught me
> not just to speak, but to think in a mother tongue
> my mother never knew, a genteel
>
> proxy for our pagan dialect
> of locked grimoires
> and backstreet skipping rhymes
>
> collective nouns
> for shore birds, new snow
> blown through the scullery door, when my mother
> sent me to fetch the coal
> on a Christmas morning.

James Joyce's *Portrait of an Artist as a Young Man* is surely not too far away, as is the epiphanic light that 'seems blessed by something other than the God/ we had to know for school', the mystery there, even then. In 'Rationing for Beginners', too, his mother waits 'with peardrops and nylons;/ my father is a gun beyond the hill,/ his shirtsleeves hemmed and seamed/ with sweet molasses', the concrete images summoning perfectly that bygone era, and the poet continues

But neither knows the childhood I will spin
from laughing gas
and mild diptheria,
the dreams I'll furnish
on the bus ride home
more gospel then I know, a house of lights

where all our yesterdays lie side by side
in narrow beds…

Philosophical considerations are embedded too – for example a the end of the poem 'Reading David Hume at the Summer Solstice, East Fife, 2019', we are encouraged to question our own 'reality' and what it consists of. Similarly, in 'Ma Bohème (after Rimbaud)', along with the overall 'Learning to Sleep' as defined in the title, the poet recalls the 'day I learned to take light for a sign/ of nothing but itself', light a theme that is threaded throughout such as 'that coldwater light' in the eyes of the girl serving breakfast which is either 'a death threat, or an effort at flirtation'.

While we are alive and able 'to bring out the dead in our hearts/ to be born again', we have no guarantee of an afterlife as shown in 'Preparations for the True Apocalypse' and we are offered an interesting perspective: 'Imagine how it looks/ when we are gone'

and everything that might have been undone
resuming, in the gaps we leave behind:
wave after wave of brightness on the land:

buckthorn and nightshade engulfing the last cracked wall,
black as the earth
in which our dreams are laid.

And let us leave him there, finding it, overall, 'sweet to be alive' – even if, along with Yeats' 'foul rag-and-bone shop of the heart', 'the heart grows frugal at the end,/ like any scavenger' – with 'the murmur of stars' not only in his 'blood' but also in his poems throughout this wonderfully achieved collection.

Patrick Lodge

Paddy Bushe: *Peripheral Vision* (Dedalus Press, 2020)
Pat Boran: Then Again (Dedalus Press, 2020)

In reviewing this collection, Bushe's suggestion to take or leave the endnotes can be helpful in allowing the poems to speak unencumbered of further explanation, or to deepen the reading of them.

Bushe is an excellent poet and the poems in this collection reflect this: '... sometimes the artist will lead you / And your amazed eyes where reason / Absolutely refuses to go' ('The Art of Belief'). Poems that seem more personal, rooted in observation, sparkle – whether the 'dance tunes of thrush and ouzel // Invisibly silvering the air from among the branches' ('The Raven's Lamentation') or those which seek to describe the impact of a musical performance. The collection's heart beats in those poems which seem of a more personal nature – about love, neighbours and friends. They are small-scale, not portentous, almost informal (though that belies the craft). Poems such as the marvellous 'Triptych for a Neighbour' and 'Afternoon Pilgrimage' are assured, persuasive and give a space in which the poem's resonances can develop and grow.

Bushe never loses a sense of humour. After heavy musing on the claims of Amergin and the Milesians' role in settling the Irish West coast, 'In a Hammock in Galicia' (dedicated to Spanish academic and Irish literature expert José Miguel Giráldez) reclaims a proper perspective for the poet, 'I laugh, not quite out loud. / The hammock sways, just a little. / Nearby, a peach drops into silence.' This is a collection well worth reading and re-reading as it reveals those moments of unexpected joy which make us human. Like Bushe we can believe it when '... below the veranda / Where our clothes, rinsed of travel dust, // Hang gratefully in the sunlight, there really is, / Shaded by the great fig tree, a lotus pond // With frogs pulsing out something important / I do not understand.' There are many highlights here in which deft, evocative writing allows for light to shine out of darkness – like at solstice when all we know is '... to gather around hope / And hold close our circled rush-lights / Finding little spurts of warmth in words.' ('Solstice').

*

The fetching cover design for *Peripheral Vision* was created by Pat Boran, another excellent Dedalus poet whose collection *Then Again* I have the unusual pleasure of reviewing here for a second time. Originally

I summarised the book in writing: 'This is an exceptional collection which rewards the reader constantly with elegant, incisive poetry whose effortless lyricism betrays the utmost craft behind it.' Are there second thoughts? Not at all. *Then Again* remains one of the highlights of 2020 and sustains a close re-reading and, indeed, reveals even more how good the writing is. The precise, stiletto-sharp images shine out as if, 'Bright lights / flash past on poles, like stylite saints / whose name we can't recall.' ('Bus Journey'). This is a collection in which the poet is fully in control of his poetry, knows what he wants to say and has the craft to do it. Yet it is not at all didactic, there is a marvellously human sense of the contingent, the contradictory within the poetry – the very title a phrase normally used to connect words that imply a contrast, an alternative perspective. The poems here can be complex, revealing themselves slowly and gracefully. Boran has the knack of making them seem simple but drawing out powerfully the purpose and point. In the best of these poems he allows us all to become voyeurs. Ostensibly many of the poems take their impetus from observed objects in museums, places or galleries but they are not really ekphrastic, except perhaps in the strictest Homeric sense where we do not need to see nor expect to see the artwork referred to. Take 'Unidentified Miracles' which is written 'after a painting attributed to Pietro Novelli in the National Gallery of Ireland' – the actual painting, which is probably of St Francis of Paola bringing back to life some fried fish (really), is largely ignored except to frame Boran's father calling him to observe something in a water-filled basin that may have been fish (or eels, or frogspawn) but the poet, and the reader, see the real miracle, not resurrected fish, but '... a sky so empty and blue/that before I knew it, it was,/in its own way too./a kind of miracle.' In the same way, perhaps, that Boran's poems draw us to view the fish but deliver something much better.

'Fountain' is as close to perfect a poem as you can get. A moment, here in Paris (the poem is dedicated to the American poet Stuart Dischell, an *aficionado* of the city), where something is seen that reveals something else that says it all. Here a receding Parisian façade stops time ('like a path in what might well have been/a woodland clearing a thousand years ago'), a drinking fountain is seen and a small bird is drinking, everyone stops 'to stand and wait our turn/a few moments more/in the history of the civilised world'. As Dischell himself had said, 'When I'm in Paris, standing on a given street corner, I can almost see the layers of history under my feet.' And Boran is well able to take such an insight and shape a precise, emotional poem around it. The poems in *Then Again* reward reading, to paraphrase Billy Collins, as if watching a mouse dropped into them, probing his way out rather than beating them with rubber hoses to find out what they really mean. 'The Big Freeze' is another poem inspired by an image – in this case probably a 1930s photo by Fr Francis Brown SJ of Titanic photographs fame – of skating seminaries, novices at being Jesuits as well as skaters. The clever references to Breughel the Elder are drawn out but, in typical leftfield fashion, Boran notes (in, possibly, an insight into his method) '…my eye is drawn to something more intense, /more telling'). With European war in the air, and now, of course, with the horrors of the invasion of Ukraine, the attention is shifted to one novice whose 'discarded great coat' is 'ominous as a body' and who skates with perfection and brio, demonstrating 'a bracket turn, / an arabesque, a perfect pirouette'. A faultless whirl of the poem from something light and observational to something of menace, and, hints of repressed physicality which tie up the close of the poem with the prefacing epigram – a marvellous circularity. The epigram refers to the lake, on the closure of the seminary in 1969, giving up its statues of classical female figures thought to have been dumped there by the Jesuits. The close of the poem develops that sense of frustrated sensuality with the lake 'scarred by the skater's blades as he goes, /unheeding of creaks, or groans, or the gentle rise/ of pockets of trapped air from deep below – /the breath of the goddesses marbling the ice.'

Boran knows the fragility of being human and alive, the tragedy and the absurdity, but his perspective is optimistic, life-affirming. Closing the wardrobe door, and the 'mirror of the self' Boran feels still 'that someone watches over me with kindness,/ the empty hangers chime inside like bells.' ('The Wardrobe'). His approach to poetry is best summed up in 'Falling' as '… the accident, the grief/somehow given grace and meaning'. Pat Boran may be not that well known this side of the Irish Sea but this collection should alter that. You will find here poems – as did the lady preparing a meal in an early Nineteenth Century Indian painting and staring into the cooking fire – that allow you to gaze '… through the moment of the task/ into some greater narrative, the larger story/of our give-and-take existences' ('A Lady Prepares a Meal'). Excellent writing.

Belinda Cooke

Eiléan Ní Chuilleanáin: *Collected Poems* (Gallery Books, 2020)

I once chanced upon *The Irish Book of Sex* in a bargain bookshop, only to discover a book of blank pages – *The Irish Book of Women Poets*, would have been as apt, judging by most Irish poetry anthologies. Yet, aside from, say, the Soviet era's public poet Anna Akhmatova, who is likely to get equal billing with Seamus Heaney, Robert Frost, Robert Lowell or W. B. Yeats? But now we have Eiléan Ní Chuilleanáin's *Collected Poems* entire, confirming her as seer with her transcendent poetry – in Maria Johnston's words: 'One could spend one's whole life reading [her] oceanic *Oeuvre* and still feel that one has only sailed on the surface of this fugitive poet's unending, elaborate, and endlessly transformative mysteries' (*Poetry Ireland Review*). Read this poetry, rich in classical myth and Ireland's folklore, its vexed history and enforced emigration and look no further – Eiléan Ní Chuilleanáin's your man.

And these 'mysteries' arise from a readily formed poetics that magically sustains fluid, elusive ideas within fixed standalone architectonic poems, leaving one grateful for the climbing ropes of Google and feminist critical texts.[1] Another Russian – Osip Mandelstam – has a comparable method which he explicates by way of Henri Bergson's[2] time philosophy, duration (*durée*) seen both as a honeycomb's network of cells, and a timeless, contemporaneous fan, spreading from a causal base. Both are perfect for visualizing Ní Chuilleanáin's rising and falling motifs as she voyages through landscapes, and seascapes, borders and boundaries, the chinks and cracks of buildings and interiors; as she encounters women's religious orders, hermits, saints and scholars, women's lives – the admired and the marginalized, with the body as symbol; on and on through music, language and translation, art, foreign travel, the mythic and the everyday, history's violence – contemporary and ancient... all just tantalizingly dangled before us to see what we can make of it. In essence, these are in the moment observations combining with erudite and diurnal thought processes, enabling the collections' shifting focuses.

---

[1] See Patricia Boyle Haberstroh, *Women Creating Women: Contemporary Irish Poets*. Dublin: Attic Press, 1996; Anne Fogarty ed., Eiléan Ní Chuilleanáin Special Issue, Irish University Press: *A Journal of Irish Studies;* Vol 37, no. 1, 2007; Lucy Collins, *Contemporary Irish Women Poets*: Liverpool Univ. Press, 2015.

[2] *Creative Evolution*. Trans. Arthur Mitchell London: Macmillan and Co. Ltd., 1913. See also Osip Mandelstam, 'Conversation about Dante' in *The Complete Critical Prose and Letters*. Trans. Jane Gary Harris, and Constance Link. Ann Arbor: Ardis, 1979.

The result for the reader is a richly intellectual and emotional experience. One sets out Googling new and eclectic subject matter, as well as fresh insights into the familiar: 'Saint' Mary Magdalene's preaching at Marseille; the nun Nano Nagle's educational work for the poor; Vercingetorix – that household name – the Celtic chieftain opposing Julius Caesar in the Gallic Wars. And one ends up sharing Ní Chuilleanáin's quiet empathy for outsiders – the girl who 'they pass... without a sound / and when they look for her face / can only see the clock behind her skull' ('The Absent Girl'); the sisters' institutionally controlled by a brother in spite of his death: 'His will, / clearly marked, and left in the top drawer, / is a litany of objects lost like itself' ('MacMoransbridge'); the broad canvas of Persian defeat of 'the poor straying barbarians' from the foot soldiers' viewpoint, there beneath the captains' lashes: 'by now their lives were nothing / but flowing away from them, breath blood and sweat' ('The Persians'). While myth – so much built in to Ní Chuilleanáin's DNA – is where mind and emotion merge the most, as in the immediacy of her narrative fragments in the prose poem 'Ag Stánadh Amach'/'Gazing Out' with its links to the Irish Epic *'Táin Bó Cualigne'/'The Cattle-raid of Cooley'*.

You can get inside this, at times elusive personal landscape by taking your time over her first collection *Acts and Monuments* (1972). Here, water comes across like a poetic manifesto – 'this water music ransacked my mind / and started it growing again in a new perspective' ('Letter to Pearse Hutchinson') – before then being juxtaposed to land: 'Water has no memory' while 'Earth remembers /facts about your relations;/... / and every stone recalls its quarry and the axe.' ('Family'). We have Odysseus battling the sea with endlessly creative, concrete images: 'he rammed / the oar between their jaws', with a shift to the demotic: 'If there was a single / streak of decency in these waves now, they'd be ridge, / pocked and was dented with the battering they've had' till finally, '...the profound / unfenced valleys of the ocean still held him' ('The Second Voyage'). Her elemental world is a place of exclusion inhabited by exiles and hermits, but it is also deliciously appealing: 'Wash man out of the earth; sheer off / the human shell. / Twenty feet down there's close cold earth / so clean' ('Wash'). She captures wonder within the domestic as in 'Swineherd', where the sinister speaker, with 'special skills', aspires to a simpler life, caught in a still life which Vermeer-like (frequently noted) has a life of its own: 'I want to lie awake at night / listening to cream crawling to the top of the jug /and the water lying soft in the cistern'.

But the collection's jewel in the crown is her nuanced lament for the plight of all exiles, 'A Midwinter Prayer'. Here, this Everyman sets out during the ancient Celtic festival of Samhain – which marks the end of harvest and onset of winter. There is a bleak accumulation of physically and psychologically cold images: 'the road stretches like the soul's posthumous journey... // and all his life seemed like a funeral journey'; a sudden shift from seasonal abundance to an unknown woman's question: 'And is that the young son / I carried through the wet and dry months?' on to a brilliantly cosmic moment: '...the girl gave birth in a ruin: / frost made angels echo behind the sky'. These fragments, enable a satisfying shift now to Everywoman, as the poem builds to a more defined universal: 'The exile is a wise man with a star and a stable; / he is an unpeopled poet staring at a broken wall.'

We have a similar collage effect in the masterly title sequence of *Site of Ambush*, her second collection. Ní Chuilleanáin's, birthplace is Cork, which, apart from Dublin, was the most active area during the War of Independence, with ambush the main tactic of the guerilla war. Given, also, her family connections with key players in the 1916 Easter Rising, one is all the more struck by her non-partisan approach. Ballad-style, sparse, visually emotive fragments give us harrowing images of both the ambushed soldiers and a child killed in the crossfire on the way to the well. The calm diction – 'dream', 'gently', 'light', settled', 'lay quiet' – is particularly chilling given the subject matter, before the dramatic shift to the awful emotive 'stacks', a horrific conjuring up of the worst of history's mass graves:

> Deafly rusting in the stream
> the lorry now is soft as a last night's dream.
> The soldiers and the deaf child
> landed gently in the water
> they were light between long weeds
> settled and lay quiet, nobody
> to listen to them now.
> The all looked the same face down there:
> water too thick and deep to see.
> ...
> A long winter stacks their bodies
> and words above their stillness hang from hooks
> in skeins, like dark nets drying,
> flapping against the stream.
> ('Narration')

'Site', rather than 'ambush' is the sequence's focus, with respect both to people and landscape. The woman alone with, 'a cropped head, / an empty face /staggers away from the sea/.../ alone remembering alone', is emblematic of many Cork women of that time, whose heads were shaved

85

both by the armed forces, as well as the IRA (for fraternization), stark lines that evoke multiple losses – personal violation, bereavement and social castigation. Here Ní Chuilleanáin also points to the poverty that may have placed the woman in this situation. From here we move to the eternal mourners: 'Now all their lives on the site of the ambush / they see the dead walking ignorant and strong / as on their dying day' – note in those telling adjectives how no word is wasted in capturing the naïve arrogance of youth and the tragedy of death in one's prime. But observe what she does with the setting then takes the whole poem off the scale, from the opening reference to the mythical 'Charybdis' both monster and whirlpool to foreshadow the impending ambush, and then in '4, Time and Place' to give a description of the world's creative force: 'Before the dead underwater shining / ...there was the scheming and streaming of the original volcanoes' set against human violence, '...Then came the clay and the raven'. Note also how these fine lines show her skill at shifting from stark, finely honed, cinematic snapshots, to beautifully sustained, open-ended lines. From here, the sequence winds to some degree of catharsis, or at least comfort, in the dream-like return of the child to its parents but transformed to a girl:

> your arms will be burnt
> as she turns to flame
> yellow on your dress
> a slight flowering tree.
>   ('Site of Ambush')

The public subject matter of the 'Site of Ambush', above, naturally leads the discussion back to this question of Ní Chuilleanáin as public poet. Yeats towards the end of his life posed a rather troubled question: 'Did that play of mine send out / Certain men the English shot?' ('Man and the Echo') which Auden then countered in his elegy, 'In Memory of W B Yeats': 'For poetry makes nothing happen'. Where along such a spectrum might Ní Chuilleanáin lie? It is clear that hers is not a simple direct oratory.

Another big profile topic is the abuse scandals among priests and religious orders, that have led to Catholic Church's loss of grace over the last few decades. Here, Ní Chuilleanáin also works in many shades of grey. All through her work, and in her recent, *The Mother House*, in particular, she tracks the meditative life of women's religious orders, setting the cloister's restricted view against its potential to be like Hamlet's words, 'bounded in a nutshell' yet 'king of infinite space'. Her study of these women's lives is just telling it how it is, at times ludicrous in its attempt to hold back from the personal, but a place of both philanthropy and innovation. But she also has poems like 'Bessboro' and 'Translation' which deal with pregnant women's incarceration. This second, describes the reburial of Magdalene women found in a convent in an unmarked grave. Here in these startling, heartbreaking lines Ní Chuilleanáin imagines the lost families of these women seeking answers to that past, as though the bones cry out with sounds of each woman's voice, merging with the very cries of their babies:

> Assist them now, ridges under the veil, shifting,
> searching for their parents, their names,
> the edges of words grinding against nature,
>
> as if, when water sank between the rotten teeth
> of soap, and every grasp seemed melted, one voice
> had begun, rising above the shuffle and hum
>
> until every pocket in her skull blared with the note –
> allow us now to hear it, sharp as an infant's cry
> while the grass takes root, while the steam rises:
> ('Translation')

At the same time, she shows that if stones are to be cast, they are not all to be thrown at the nuns – the society, the families that rejected pregnant daughters, the men who abandoned them, the public which knew all about it, were at least as much responsible. It is just magic the way she lets language do this job for her as the poem winds to its conclusion, where the girls in the laundries and the nuns who ran them are, to a degree, now ranged together against the powers outside their control. Could the newly-named novice have imagined such a 'parasitic' role when she took up her vocation? How long have the Magdalenes, and their families (and, indeed, society) all had to bear the weight of these keys on so many levels:

> the baked crust
> of words that made my temporary name.
> a parasite that grew in me. That spell
> lifted. I lie in earth sifted to dust.
> let the bunched keys I bore slacken and fall.
> I rise and forget. a cloud over my time.

If Ní Chuilleanáin's is indeed a public voice, then surely it is a voice of healing – if society can make amends, then all should be allowed to rest. Elma

Mitchell's poem 'This Poem is Dangerous', gives a pertinent take on poetry's power to influence, with something that comes close to what Ní Chuilleanáin can give us, in a way that allows such inclusion for all: 'All poems must carry a Government warning. Words / can seriously affect the heart.'

Patrick Lodge

Gerard Smyth: *The Sundays of Eternity* (Dedalus Press, 2020)
Mary O'Donnell: *Massacre of the Birds* (Salmon Poetry, 2020)

This is a collection with a strong note of positivity from a very prolific poet (this is his tenth collection) looking backwards across seventy years. He may write ('Burning the Manuscripts') of the 'whole songbook of my youth' being consumed in an exuberant blaze but the memories linger and animate many of the poems here. It is as well that 'I found them again, treasures that were lost –' ('*XXX*') and the gentle tone of the collection very much has, indeed, the feel of 'love letters sent to an old address' ('*XXX*'). The sequence 'Riddling the Ashes' is characteristically wry in exploring a life whose origins in the 1950s/1960s would tend to place them in the category of ancient history for many contemporary readers, a house of memories 'where those who lived in its sanctuary / never asked for more than they had'. It is a world of the uneventful, where unnerved children are 'sent to fetch a can of milk, a block of butter / six hen eggs in their cardboard cups' ('Saint Swithin's Day'). Photographs too encourage a reflection on the genetic inheritance, the 'resemblance / between those in that moment and your face' ('The Sepia Years'). There are several poems focused on courtship and marriage which, though measured and calm, are also lyrical and passionate – and as such speak strongly of the strengths of Smyth as a poet. He is right to note that 'There are scenes that belong to the bliss of memory' ('The Given Chance') and these scenes are beautifully measured out including the delightful 'Wedding Night in Westport'. One imagines there are many things to be recalled about a wedding night but the poem is typical of Smyth's ability to reveal so much by a slightly askew perspective and a telling eye for the detail that, like an iceberg tip, only hints at the depths of which it is a part – 'The linen needed a puff of your perfume / to remove the scent of previous guests'. Indeed, in this 'house of bygones / everything has been kept' ('From Room to Room') and this is a collection given its considerable emotional heft by reminiscence but also by the recognition of things passing, 'A young bride's face, dulled by time / is pressed to the glass of a photo-frame.'('From Room To Room').

The range of subjects within the collection is wide. Poems reference, *inter alia*, the cellist, Jacqueline Du Pré, 'our neighbourhood misfits' the local Teddy Boys and Trump. 'War Poets' is competent but unremarkable yet is immediately redeemed by the elegiac 'Drinking Wine in France' where the life in Ireland of the poet, Francis Ledwidge, killed in action in July

1917, is recalled with lightness and grace. It is a masterful poet whose final lines softly prefigure Ledwidge's fate as he cycles to '…the beguiling bog / and to the hilltop where every year / the dead increased their tenure'. Smyth isn't one for grandstanding in his poetry – his effects are achieved by acute observation, a lyricism and an eye for the decisive detail. It is the extraordinariness within the ordinary which he sees clearly – perfectly expressed in the female actor who delivers a stunning Antigone but still, 'She checks her loose change for the bus / Remembers what she forgot to put / on her supermarket shopping list.'('Playhouse'). The lovely 'Waterloo Sunrise' may suggest the Kinks but the sense of carefully observed vignettes unrolling at twenty four frames per second is more Romantic film than Rock 'n Roll. This is a pleasant collection to read, swirling with music and the sounds of bells; a collection of a poet who is comfortable in himself and his art. It starts with a Heaney epigram asking the question 'How perilous is it to choose / Not to love the life we're shown?' and Smyth has clearly taken this to heart and, indeed, shares with us his contemplation on a life loved.

*

When a reviewer describes an author as 'prolific' there is sometimes a hint that quality has been replaced by quantity. When a publisher's blurb focuses on the large range of subject matter covered by the poems in a collection, there is sometimes a hint that there is not much else to say about them. Well, Mary O'Donnell is a prolific writer and poet and the breadth of subject matter covered in this latest collection is very wide indeed, but both here are causes for celebration as another collection by a poet writing at the top of her game. The breadth of her insights is only matched by the quality of the poetry that expresses them. O'Donnell is able to write persuasively and graciously about whatever animates her as a poet, be it personal or otherwise – thus there are powerful poems about refugees which both lament the inhumanity of their situation but also accord the individuals a dignity and a hopefulness. 'On the lakeshore of living conscience / I stand // I can do no other' she writes in 'Against The Vanishing' and the collection proves her determination to speak out honestly about the world she lives in and its injustices. The precision of her language and imagery throughout suggest she writes with a scalpel rather than a pen. O'Donnell never hammers home a point but gently caresses it into its rightful place on the page. Even in the moving series of poems about her mother, O'Donnell remains a consummate poet exploring ageing with no sentimentality, merely love and an honest recognition of what is happening. Across the piece O'Donnell seems to derive support from the natural world – as Emerson put it, the land is 'tranquilizing and sanative'. Thus, 'The Dumpster', about clearing a relative's effects, ends, 'She is eight months dead. / Hedges and birdsong extol the day'.

'I marvel at the power of women' she writes in 'Mother, I am Crying', and there are several poems which boil with righteous anger at the treatment of women. 'It Wasn't A Woman', with its litany of male crimes against women, and '#Me Too, 12 Remembered Scenes and a Line', with its list of the sexual assaults and harassments suffered by the poet as everywoman (with its damning, ironic ending, 'I was not raped'), are clear about the world in which women grow and develop. They are fiercely polemical but always underpinned by a lyrical and acute awareness of being a woman and a human being. There is tough stuff here, sometimes remorseless, but O'Donnell also shows a lighter side – the marvellous 'Sandals' uses a purchase many years ago in Camden of red leather sandals to riff on the joy of simply being alive '…as I moved past the crates / of oranges, persimmons, bright red peppers'. In 'A Poem from Gotland', O'Donnell references the Bataclan terrorist attack and wonders, while she will 'survive the night as the young are murdered', how it is possible to contemplate writing: 'Tomorrow it's hard to believe / That I can try to write again / Or any of us'. As the American poet, Robert Duncan, put it, 'the poet's role is not to oppose evil but to imagine it'. We should all be grateful that O'Donnell does both in this outstanding collection and all the while remaining a consummate and humanitarian craftswoman.

Duncan Sprott

In loco parentis

James Harpur: *The Examined Life* (Two Rivers Press, 2021)

Anyone settling down with *The Examined Life* in the hope of finding more of James Harpur's erudite musings upon the lives of the saints may be in for… a big surprise: he has ditched his trademark spiritual exercises in favour of his own schooldays. Thus the examined life: a life full of, ruled by, exams – jest – but also, of course, in serious allusion to Socrates and 'the unexamined life is not worth living'.

One's initial reaction might be: one has had quite enough of schooldays, one's own memories thereof. Or, has not this territory – rich kids behaving badly – already been thoroughly trampled and done to death? But the answer is that to read these fine poems has a similar effect to reading Karl Ove Knausgaard: one is led to compare one's own experiences with his; and that nobody has dealt with the microcosm of school quite like this.

Harpur kicks off with an epigraph from *Tom Brown's Schooldays*, about telling the truth and keeping a brave and kind heart, and never listening to or saying anything you wouldn't have your mother and sister hear; and another from the *Odyssey*: 'Oh no! What is this land I've come to? Will the inhabitants be violent, wild and cruel, or god-fearing and welcoming to strangers?' The world the thirteen-year-old Harpur is exiled to is the gulag of the English public school, in his case, Cranleigh, where *every* species of inhabitant may be found. Like any new boy, Harpur is at first overawed and dismayed. But if he finds some enemies he also makes plenty of friends, refuses to succumb to homesickness and will stay the course. The quotation from Thomas Hughes is ironic, for, his own brave, kind heart notwithstanding, Harpur has fallen among rough boys good at swearing, some of whom are 'thugs and sadists', the sort of boys who will tip a chap out of his bed in the middle of the night.

From the start there is a heightened sense of light and dark: the master doesn't switch off the dormitory lights but 'switches on the dark'. When Harpur talks about a blackboard 'with darkness just a wipe away' he's also talking about life. *Life*, too, can tip you out of bed and switch on the dark. Thus the leitmotif for Harpur's collection, for we can perceive in these graphic, meticulously wrought pages the actual process of education, of growing up, of grappling with life.

Harpur mines a rich seam of memory, giving us vibrant poems about dormitory life and its terrors (such as being assailed by match-flicking shades bent on setting your hair on fire); about his separating parents ('the two of them re-glued/ for just an hour or so'); about the school's private lingo (*moab*, *doof*, *razzer*); about his 'bad' brother 'Monty' (who drives away a tank on army open day); about bullies; about sex education ('Please, Miss, can you show us your tits?'); about the 'Harpies' who snatch his food (in the matter of doughnuts Harpur is a Harpy himself); about an out-of-bounds escapade to a pub on the back of Monty's motorbike; about a fire-drill, in which he compares the school to a sinking liner; and about away matches and the risqué songs sung on the way back ('Oh she's got a lovely *bottom*... set of teeth').

Much of this is ingeniously (re-)viewed through the filter of Homer, in whose works Harpur has steeped himself – we can now see – all his life. For example, 'The Housemaster's Enchanting Wife' is another Circe, who serves 'a fragrant brew of wine, and a pernicious drug to makes us utterly forget our homes... she tapped us with her wand/ and turned us into pigs...' In 'Fifteen Minutes' getting downstairs to breakfast is like going into battle: 'The first alarum marmalises sleep/ and from a tent of dreams I see the siege/ is just the same: Trojans look like Greeks/ and the dead rise up, their eyelids glued/ stretching arms as if to break a cage.' He continues with: 'At camp again I fit my armoured shirt,/ quiver my mind with arrows, put on greaves.' And then:

> The breakfast bell sets off a cussing chaos
> and the stairs cascade with coltish hooves –
> I duck and weave like Paris, primed to kill,
> rehearsing every boy's Achilles Heel.

In 'Mum's First Letter' Harpur has been 'At sea for days and casting memories/ overboard I heard the Sirens call/ and lure me to the rocks of images/ of old September evenings...' He jettisons memory – like ballast – to stop being capsized by thoughts of home: 'I blocked my ears, and tied up to a mast... until at last/ the song was drowned by distance... and the wind/ being strangled in the rigging.' In place of Lotus-eaters Harpur wants 'to stay forever with the Crisp Eaters,/ keep munching crisps, munching crisps'. And in 'Breaking Up', when Harpur arrives home he puts on scruffy clothes 'and looks for clues/ of my old life, like Odysseus in his palace/ disguised as a beggar.' Of Neggers, his Latin master, Harpur says 'He skippered me through the *Odyssey*/ each line a wave that led to Ithaca.' The same might be said of Harpur's poems, many of which lead us back to Homer, and to re-examine our own Ithacas. Harpur, of course, never writes anything by accident: we're meant to pick up his hints, meant to enter the labyrinth – or maze – that he has cunningly built, and to share the delights and horrors of the journey of this latterday Telemachus/ Odysseus.

For Harpur, trying to come to terms with his parents' split-up, has cast himself as Telemachus – the boy waiting for his father's return, though in Harpur's case he knows that his father has left home for good. At the start, home is Ithaca, the place he doesn't want to leave, and school itself stands *in loco parentis*, with the Head 'as though he were my father'. It's as if by going to boarding school he's gotten his dad back. Throughout, Harpur wrestles with the idea of a father, his absent father, and his relations with that father, who, driving off, is 'my *pater ex machina*/ dropping facial tics/ of unsaid words like litter/ at a picnic'. Five years later, the new intake of boys will look at Harpur himself 'as if I were their dad'. If Harpur's father is an errant Odysseus, his mother with her unfinished tapestry is another Penelope, albeit, as Harpur says, one with no suitors. If Harpur's – sometimes painful – portrayal of his parents seems less than generous, through wry adolescent eyes, it should be noted that in his previous work (e.g. in the sonnet sequence *The Frame of Furnace Light*), he gives them far more kindly treatment.

The Examined Life is Harpur's longest sequence of interlinked poems, something which allows him to weave – *passim* – a tight web of words, with elaborate internal echoes and interlacings. It is fitting that he should reach for photographic metaphors, for what he has given us here is an album of candid snapshots, scalpel-sharp glimpses of his past, stills that also come to life, their themes sparking and ricocheting in all directions like a box of fireworks. Nothing here is less than memorable: strip lights are 'like long iced buns'; of a fire escape he says 'we clatter down meccano stairs'; in a leaver's prank a flag is raised and 'flick flick flickers/ catches the breeze and flutters/ into a pair/ of lacy black knickers'.

While Harpur has a lot of fun with Homer, he hates school and his allusions are often funereal: on the first day he and his father get out of the car 'as calm as undertakers'; cars delivering boys at the start of term are a 'cortège'; on his last day, trunks lifted into boots are 'coffin-heavy'. If Cranleigh is a living death, another Hades, complete with ghosts in the night, it is also 'Colditz', where the masters are 'goons', and the boys 'prisoners'.

For Socrates the unexamined human life was one deprived of the meaning and purpose of existence. To become fully human, he said, means to use our highly developed faculty of thought to raise our existence above that of mere beasts. Harpur has fun with this too: it's as if nothing matters at Cranleigh except exam results. One half suspects that Harpur uses the idea as his justification for breaking rules, for he does plenty of that, smoking, boozing, adventures out of bounds, and so on.

Harpur finds a friend for life, wilfully referred to throughout as 'me and Jonesy', who is almost in loco parentis himself, a kind of stand-in for the all but redundant pair, 'me and Mum' and the unmentioned 'me and Dad'. Of Jonesy he says:

I saw my other self at once.
Each day like hostages we dreamt
of anywhere beyond the now and here
of unexamined lives worth living.

Their world is one of border-guards, protocol, bullies in 'sleek-suited SS black' and *careless emotion costs lives.*' All rather like re-living a war, not only Troy but also World War II, *the* war. At Cranleigh, everything is a battle. A sunset is 'like the Thin Red Line at Balaclava'; the beds are 'Crimean'. The end-of-term mood is 'demob euphoric'. The military metaphor continues in 'Love Letter', where Harpur makes himself 'invulnerable/ to verbal bullets shrapnel mortar fire/ flying around the trenches of the school.' He feels his girlfriend's love illuminate his face – 'as if I've struck/ a match and tensed a hundred snipers' hands/ on the darker side of no-man's land.' This balances the lit matches flipped earlier. Here, though, the lighted match is not about hate but the healing light of love.

In 'His Father's Ghost', Harpur feels that his father, having dumped him at school, and having abandoned the family home, might just as well *be* a ghost and thinks of the ghost of Aeneas' father in Hades – which his son 'tried to hug three times/ but thrice his arms went through the ghost – as if it were a breeze, or fleeting dream.' In the second part, Harpur sees not his own father's ghost but his fifteen-year-old self wrestling with his Virgil prep – and wants to give him the hug that his father would or could not. He imagines the young Harpur going 'to sleep/ perchance to dream and roam the underworld/ and search the Styx and Cocytus/ for the shade of a father/ in loco parentis.'

Another major preoccupation is sleep. In 'Middle Dormitory: Passover', sleepers are like the dead: 'A stationary ghost train/ sometimes a boy might spring up from a nightmare/ and jabber on then sink back to his coffin...' Not only are beds compared to coffins but 'four shades appear/and tilt a bed up... a boy-cum-mattress crumpled to the floor,/ his piggy grunts converging to a cry.' Harpur prays to be saved, holds his breath, then feels them pass him by: 'returning to the dark from which they'd crept/ the corner of your sleep that never slept.' At the end of his schooldays he will feel as if he's been holding his breath for the entire five years.

One feels some sympathy for the vividly-drawn matron with her 'tent-peg nose' and 'the trapdoor laugh of a marionette' who 'shoots out like Scylla from her lair/ to savage us about laundry, dirty clothes'. Matron, who, when she waylays Harpur to talk to him, is mercilessly mocked by the other boys making 'horrific pelvic thrusts behind her back'. Harpur adds to the mockery, with a remark about 'her bum the size of Canada' (*De mortuis nil nisi bonum?*). For their visit to Matron's 'lair' to watch Jonesy's actor father on her television, Harpur and Jonesy become 'two oleaginous angels' – 'the sons she never mothered'. Matron is recast not only as a stray from the *Odyssey* but is also hauled into service as an extra surrogate parent. She, too, is in loco parentis.

Day boys are compared to helots – serfs or slaves – who are like 'our shadows'. Their eyes 'soft with comforts filled us with dismay.' 'Invisible by day, at night/ they lived in full/ the half-forgotten life we hoped to live in school.' Always, Harpur wants out.

Even a dayboy has his uses, though. In 'A Midsummer's Night', Harpur and Jonesy commandeer a helot to bring them 'a penitential offering'. The helot's day-boy sins are absolved, and the dream – of escape – is made to come (briefly) true in the shape of 'twelve cans of pissy beer' and Gauloises in a cornfield, nicely fitted into a military context of crossing borders, parachute drop, the Maquis, jumping at every noise 'as if the field's concealing a regiment of masters' and sneaking past prefects in guardrooms: all crisply (re-)observed – 'a scooter's whine/ mosquito-loud' 'our cigarette tips flitting/the dark like fire flies'.

'Cleaners' treats of the 'Jims', an underclass of left behind-ers, below even the Helots, rejects in the game of life, who are rumoured to have 'escaped from loony-bins', and whom Harpur calls 'almost human beings'. But he also says 'They came to be like family/ as long as it wasn't your own'. What he calls: 'a secret everybody/ pretended he didn't know' – 'the scrawny negatives/ of scholars, rugby heroes,/ blacked-out images/that popped up in the holidays/ like Reggie, with his violent shakes'. The secret is that the 'Jims' are just like everybody else: actual real humans.

In a poem about chapel: 'Stanford's *Jubilate* shakes the air:/ we sing like lions, a pride of one/ primeval roar – five hundred gentlemen/ like chanting Millwall skinheads at the Den'. Tyche alone – Luck – has allowed Harpur his elite education; change but the names and circs. and he might have ended up as a Millwall skinhead himself, or mopping corridors like the 'Jims'. As it is, Harpur dubs his fellow pupils 'red-pocked beasts of saurus species', 'skin-clad tribes', and 'grunting hogs with bristly hides', who speak 'a pidgin of refined obscenity'.

Some readers might take offence at this obscenity, but if Harpur lets off a bit of linguistic steam, he deserves credit for telling it How it Was. Boys are like this: they do swear. Thus 'We wish the chapel bell would just sod off ' and 'Hurry up' 'Piss off' 'No *you* piss off', and the prefects of the Rapax legion (the nickname of the XXIst, 'Grasping') caw 'pass the *fucking* ketch'. Even Harpur's bad language is of the very highest order.

The conceit of 'Plato's Cave' that it's not the real world outside school but an illusion, from which one boy escapes and returns to tell what reality was really like, having crawled through darkness to the entrance and seen: 'the 1970s! – a giant disco dance/ of long-haired folk in pink crushed velvet loons, embroidered kaftans, bangles, platform shoes… where people kissed and dressed in rainbow light/ But all we knew was grey, or black and white./ They chained him up again; we shut our eyes/ and blocked our ears, and felt our teens slip by.'

Half way through the book school begins almost to feel more like home than home itself, a haven, and Harpur is counting the hours till the new term begins. School almost replaces Harpur's actual home as (one of) his Ithaca(s).

In 'Dance' the Cranleigh boys do escape their cave, though, and get to meet *'real live girls* in party dresses' ('For unlike Gaul, Girl was still *terra incognita'*) – girls who 'with swirly eyes inspect us all/ like cases on an airport carousel…' Harpur feels 'the pressure of an O level/ to crack a joke with every phrase/ and grade myself by every giggle'. Even a girls' school dance is an exam. 'Dance' is great stuff, in which Harpur lets rip, with: '*Our Nobby of Gymnasium*/ his sculpted bum in skin-tight jeans,/ no longer bodyguard but Bacchus – /his clean-cut National Service grin/ a beatific ooze of sex/ as he boogies with the mistress to T-Rex.'

Having more or less given up his Dad for lost, in 'Prof', when Harpur's girlfriend's father, a surgeon, is blown up by an IRA car-bomb, it's as if he has lost not a potential father-in-law but an actual parent. 'I felt as if I'd lost a dad/ *again* – the listener/ I'd never really had;/ a soulful empathiser.' Odyssean shipwreck is everywhere. The striking thing here is the prof's magnanimity, and the words on his memorial: 'It/ matters not how a man dies/ but how he lives'.

One might think that the young Harpur, planning a trip to France, would opt for, say, Notre Dame, Chartres, Vézelay. Not a bit of it: Harpur the pilgrim and mystic does not yet exist. In 'Furies' he and Jonesy hitch to Nice and St Tropez, ending up on the (topless) beach at Cannes.

By the time Harpur reaches the sixth form, the sleeping boys in 'Taking prayers in the Junior Dormitory: First Night' ('boys as peaceful as they were in wombs/ lie dreamless as dogs on medieval tombs') have become 'horrid pupae/ I cannot wait to never see again'. He has had enough of the

Spartan regime with 'open toilets voyeur baths'. He wants to be off on his own voyage, not marooned on the island of school, not playing Telemachus stuck at home with his mother.

A game of squash is the focus for Harpur's collapse with glandular fever and his temporary removal from school. He has felt like a prisoner at Cranleigh, yet now he's to be sent home sick he doesn't want to go home at all. He is driven not only by the urge to win at games but has set his heart on the agon of getting into Cambridge. Recovered, he is another Lazarus 'edging/ towards dazzle and bird roar'. On the way back to school he walks into a pub that's full of his pals: 'they turn and cheer/ as if I'm a lifer sprung from jail.' He goes on: 'I sip my pint of Bass, salute/ my glad captains…' 'And taste the grief/ that soon we'll be at home for good/ and filing into/ the orphanage of life.'

At one point the threat of expulsion for smoking hangs over Harpur. A master brings the verdict 'doubtful – as if he's poised/ to give an LBW decision./ His words could finish my career. / My life. But he declares 'Not out!…' Harpur is 'an *Oxbridge angel*, un-ex-pellable, a sacred life form', trailing clouds of glory.

By the time he is eighteen his attitude has changed utterly: leaving school he feels like a man about to have his head cut off. Now that he must bid farewell to his comrades he realises the war is over. In *Ithaca* he says: 'and now I feel that same dismay/ the quiver in my mother's lip/ a sudden leap of distancing/ as when Odysseus left Penelope / not knowing what to say to her; / or maybe when on leaving Troy / and bound for Ithaca – a home/ he'd see afresh with eyes of war – / he put his baffled hands on / shoulders/ of comrades he'd never see again./ *Amen.*'

Though he never uses the word, Harpur's book is *all about* the Homeric *nostos*, homecoming, about finding where home is, when home is not quite home. Forty years later, he and Jonesy are still nostalgic for school 'like beret-wearing veterans', eager to re-live anything they can.

In place of his parents, then, Harpur got Harpies, Helots, Circe, Scylla, and Sirens (though, oddly, no Cyclops). The imaginary is not only a template for this poet's life, but for any life. We are all Telemachuses, Odysseuses or Penelopes: we are all Homers too – not only tellers of stories, but also voyagers. *The Examined Life* is a fine reminder of the universality of Homer, and it gives Harpur himself a kind of universality, even though his own odyssey – bar a few trips to other schools to play games, and that excursion to 'wine-dark France' – has taken him precisely nowhere. It may also be Harpur's triumph, a true 'memory palace', by turns serious and hilarious, touching and shocking, relentlessly clever, full of *fun* and *mischief.* In piecing together, like the tesserae of a glittering mosaic, these disparate fragments of memory, Harpur has made his own past sing.

Angels on each Leaf

Patricia McCarthy interviews James Harpur about his recent collection, *The Oratory of Light: Poems in the Spirit of St Columba,* Wild Goose Publications (www.ionabooks.com).

James Harpur has published eight books of poetry and won a number of awards, including the Michael Hartnett Poetry Prize and the UK National Poetry Competition. His debut novel, *The Pathless Country,* a spiritual quest set in early-20th century Ireland and London, was published in 2021 by Cinnamon Press. He is a member of Aosdána, the Irish academy of the arts, and lives in the wilds of West Cork. www.jamesharpur.com

P McC: James, what originally sparked off your abiding interest in old Celtic Saints? Quite a while back, you brought out a more general little book on them, didn't you?

JH: I suspect all poets / artists seek an 'otherness' in their lives and art, both as a relief from the quotidian grind of the ego but also as a place in which to express a world view, or personal things that would be too raw if tackled head on. For some reason the medieval world has been an otherness for me, along with related areas, such as myth and mysticism. Saints, particularly the Celtic ones, are strange ambivalent figures that appeal to my imagination. Tertullian is supposed to have said something like *credo quia absurdum*, and it's the *absurda* of hagiographies, usually dismissed by historians, that fascinate me. I have in mind the story of St Kevin praying with his arms outstretched for such a length of time that a blackbird laid an egg on one of his palms; or Brendan landing his coracle on an island and lighting a fire then finding the island suddenly moving (it turns out to be a whale); or St Gobnait finding her predicted final resting place at the sign of nine white deer emerging from a forest. These images are of the stuff of the imagination that Blake, Coleridge, Yeats and Hughes, among others, would have recognised; and they are like flames to my wee moth-like sensibility. Since you ask, I did have a section on Irish saints in my book *The Dark Age* (Anvil, 2007), which also includes a long poem on Symeon Stylites, the Syrian 'pillar' saint, who spent most of his life living on top of a high column in the middle of the desert. He's a brilliant example of humanity stripped to its essence, degraded yet holy, presumptuous yet humble (and, remarkably, the base of his column can still be seen).

P McC: And now this little/big book, focusing on St Columba, or Columcille. I remember at school in Ireland when I was about nine learning all about his

great influence in spreading Christianity. Your Preface is very illuminating as to how and why you conceived of the collection that you began writing during the Covid pandemic, the restrictions imposed taking you 'to the imaginative freedom of the island of Iona...' What was or is it about Iona and Columba's life that appealed to you so much?

JH: Interesting to hear that you learned about Columba at school (or rather, as you say, Columcille, his Irish name, meaning 'dove of the church') – I don't think schools bruit his name so loudly now! For me Columba and Iona, where he founded his famous monastery, seemed to present a holy and holistic realm in which everything – human beings, animals, and nature – had its place and was subject to divine laws. Prayer, prophecy and clairvoyance, visions and dreams, spiritual healing and synchronistic encounters were not considered freakish. Angels and demons were real presences. It's said Columba himself exorcised a pail of milk in which a demon was residing, and saw, clairvoyantly, a monk who was thatching a roof fall towards the ground but caught at the last moment by an angel. Now we find our superheroes with special powers on computer screens, but in Columba's day they apparently could be found in the human realm; and this belief in the possibility of miracles appeals to me because it's analogous to the infinite possibilities of the imagination, which is, after all, the foundation of all poetry. Also, purely on the level of psychic health, it's important to me to honour a view of life that challenges our mainstream scientism and rationalism. World is suddener and more crazy than we think. Sometimes we need oxygen tents of impossibility to avoid suffocation by a system that posits relentless cause and effect.

On a broader theme, scientific advances have changed the perception of the poetic / mythic imagination (and its manifestation in myth, legend, folklore and poetry) – from a bearer of spiritual or symbolic truths to a purveyor of picturesque or whimsical fables. It's similar to the fate of holy wells after the Reformation – from oases of healing to kitsch 'wishing wells'. I feel aligned to Yeats's view that we no longer see 'in the rainbow the still bent bow of a god thrown down in his negligence ...' Jung, too, said that science had 'dehumanised our world' and made us feel emotionally distant from natural events. I often feel this distance myself, acutely, and remember Blaise Pascal, looking at the night sky and exclaiming: 'The eternal silence of these infinite spaces terrifies me': the 'heavens' and the music of the spheres had become 'outer space' with its flotillas of dead rocks.

So, in short, as an antidote to all this, I found the life of Columba on Iona a reminder of the spiritual and symbolically resonant world we've largely lost, but which, with the right imagination, is still there, waiting for us to return. I still remember my first visit to Iona and how the boat across the narrow sound from Mull delivered me to what George MacLeod, the founder of the Iona Community, described as a 'a "thin place" – only a tissue paper separating the material from the spiritual'. Iona, like Cavafy's 'Ithaca', is a state of mind as much as a physical place.

P McC: Would I be right in saying that, in this meditative collection, you take new directions in various ways: there is a real narrative drive to the poems, with direct speech, and your use of the persona of a Columban monk to narrate at various points works well in conjuring the reality of that community at the time. Secondly you skilfully merge your own poems with your versions of Old Irish poems – is this your first time as a translator / version-maker?

JH: I think the collection *is* a bit different to others I've done – in ways I was unable to predict at the outset; and it might be that the book's impetus, tone and method did have something to do with the first Covid lockdown when suddenly the traffic ceased, the aeroplanes left no feathery scars on the blue vellum of the skies, and neighbours emerged to greet each other like shy deer from a forest. It was an otherworld in itself, and perhaps that created a longing in me to perpetuate this 'recovered Eden' via an imaginative recreation of sixth-century Iona. As for the narrator, at first I imagined I would be a modern-day outsider describing events on medieval Iona; but the first poems of the book were versions from anonymous Old Irish verse ascribed to Columba, and they got me used to writing in the first person from the point of view of Columba or one of his monks. These Old Irish poems are simple and poignant, and they struck the key note for me. Part of one of them, for example, has these lines:

By the Abbey of Durrow
The elms are whispering ...
And in the startle of a flurry
A blackbird sings.

At dawn in Ross Grencha
I hear the stags; and cuckoos
At the tremble of summer
Blow echoes through the woods.
(from 'Nostos')

We live in a world of noise – from traffic to refrigerator hum – and the example above emphasises the delicacy of natural sounds – the elms, the flurry of wings, the belling of stags, the call of the cuckoo. Again, going back to the first lockdown, it was possible once again to hear more easily, and more welcomingly, the little creatures of nature (I live in the country) reasserting their small voices.

You ask whether it's my first time as a translator / version-maker – sadly, no! I've had a good few attempts at translating things over the years, most coherently, perhaps, in a book called *Fortune's Prisoner*, the poems of Boethius from his *Consolation of Philosophy* (Anvil Press, 2007), but also stabs at bits of Homer, Virgil, Horace and Dante, plus the odd Anglo-Saxon riddle, and a bit of modern Greek. I'm actually hopeless at modern languages – I seem to be forever stuck in a limbo of O Level French, for example, no matter how hard I try to get better. A language usually has to be at least a thousand years dead before I can tackle it. Moving targets are the problem.

P McC: With the mélange of different voices in the book, can I ask: have you ever thought of producing this work on a stage?

JH: I've never thought of that possibility, but it's a seductive idea and it *might* work – perhaps a stylised drama like a medieval mystery or miracle play? If there are any theatre directors reading this – do get in touch with my people (aka me)!

P McC: In your sparse yet meditative verse forms you manage to wed craft to meaning – can you say something about the way you chose the forms you wrote in?

JH: In terms of poetic technique I decided I had to go for something 'non-literary' in style, that is to say verse that is pared-down and with simple diction, partly to blend in with my versions of the Old Irish poems but also to create or preserve the sixth-century atmosphere. Poems are always aiming to create an enchantment, a world unto themselves, and temptingly ingenious metaphors or imagery can break the spell. The spell I wanted to cast was that of early medieval Iona and I felt too much literary sophistication, or perhaps literary self-consciousness, would puncture it. One always has to be humble to the content of the work and to resist cleverness for its own sake. So I tried to use simple forms of rhyme and rhythm for the most part, including sonnets and ballads. At the back of my mind were Blake's 'Songs of Innocence' and the folk verse, rhymes and spells collected in Alexander Carmichael's *Carmina Gadelica*.

P McC: This collection – with its seemingly simple language, its seemingly simple presentation on pure white paper, beautifully produced in signatures and not perfect bound, with wood engravings and other images by Paul Ó Colmáin for the cover and section openers – is like a miraculous vision in itself. Can you say a bit about the process of production and collaboration?

JH: Thank you, Patricia, it's kind of you to say that, though with your Irish blood and love of myth and legend (I'm thinking of your Tristan and Iseult cycle) you are probably my Platonic form of a reader! I am lucky to know the artist Paul Ó Colmáin, who lives near me in West Cork and is not only a wonderful artist but also a gifted poet, musician and Irish language teacher. We found out that we both shared an enthusiasm for Irish culture and heritage and have had plans, for a while, to produce a book of poems and images focusing on Irish saints. Once I had started writing my Columba poems it was natural to get in touch with Paul and see if he would produce a bevy of telling images to complement the text. It's not an 'illustrated book' as such, but Paul's scattering of engravings and drawings adds a crucial dimension to the words. We were also lucky to have such a sympathetic publisher in Sandra Kramer and her team at Wild Goose Publications, based in Scotland, who specialise in spiritual and meditative books with a Celtic, and specifically an Iona, flavour. The book seems to have been a labour of love all around, and all labours of love are no labours at all.

P McC: Your musical ear is faultless in these poems – with their rhythms, assonance, sibilance, repetition (like Taliesin in 'Dies Irae', plus the echoes of Latin), rhyming couplets – and even a sense of 'Jack and Jill' in your 'Ballad of the Milk Vessel'. Which music most inspires you, and do you play any musical instrument?

JH: I can manage a few chords on the guitar, just enough to be able to warble the odd tune and to appreciate that, alas, I have little talent as a guitarist. But music has always been part of my family. Back in the day the Harpurs were harp players who arrived in Ireland in the wake of Strongbow's Anglo-Norman invasion in 1169. The form of my name is a contraction of 'Harpour', and was the Norman French for a harp player. In some medieval Dublin records there are listed names such as Geoffrey le Harpur and Philippus le Harpur. Over time the 'le' got dropped as the Harpurs morphed into ordinary citizens with or without their specialist talent. But it gives me a huge pleasure to take out my Irish passport and see a golden harp emblazoned on the cover! And I have vowed that if there is another lockdown I'll buy a harp and channel the ancestors. As for music that inspires me ... I like bits of everything from almost every genre. Music that is otherworldly, harmonious and suggestive of another reality would be my favourite – Tallis, Tavener, Bach, Orthodox liturgy, the Corpus Christi Carol, spring to mind; I have an unexpected love of Mahler – his Ninth Symphony moves me to the point that I can't listen to it. Brahms's *Requiem* was an early love. Sibelius's violin concerto a recent love. Richard Strauss has sudden chord shifts that make me tingle. And, of course, the Beatles.

P McC: Then there are many sacred images in the book, some repeated such as the 'soul' and 'angels'. I loved, for example, in your version of an Old Irish poem, the delicacy of the vision of ancient Derry with 'the angels on each leaf / of every oak tree'. The spirituality is intense – is it yours?

JH: Yes, that image of Derry is lovely all right – I can say that with impunity because it isn't mine but that of the anonymous Irish poet who wrote it. It's an unexpected image – the angels giving the oak tree not only a golden aura but also a sense of lightness in each leaf, and a sense that each leaf is protected and individual, yet part of a whole. On top of that, the poem is a reminder that 'Derry' is derived from the Irish *Doire*, meaning an oak grove, and that the region of Derry, along with Donegal, was special to Columba (who was born in nearby Donegal and founded a monastery in Derry). It's a good example of how the poetic imagination works on many levels.

As for the spirituality of the book, it goes without saying that Columba's world was intensely spiritual, especially from our modern point of view, and it's a world that part of me hankers for. I find myself at odds with almost anything 'modern' or technological, from multi-storey car parks (my best image of soullessness) to internet banking and call centres (my idea of Dantean purgatory). Also, I have to confess there is a lot of spiritual DNA in me; my father's family have had Church of Ireland clerics in almost every generation; and my mother's family have had a long association with more esoteric Yeats-style spirituality. I was raised to believe that the invisible realm was a natural one. Experiences of my own have also shaped my religious outlook, and I have explored these in various books, especially the title poem of my last book, *The White Silhouette* (Carcanet, 2018) and in my debut novel, *The Pathless Country* (Cinnamon, 2021). So the Columba poems are really an amalgam of Columba's and my own experiences – but always using the stories of his life as a starting point and being as faithful to them as possible.

P McC: Some wonderful , delicate and beautiful lines would seem to relate to your own poetry e.g. in 'Columba the Scribe':

The rhythm of my quill
  Lets pages drink
  Wisdom in ink

There are, too, lessons for all of us as in 'The Pattern of the Day':

Allow the spirit to guide your hand
And soften your speech: live life
As if you're on the verge of singing

Would you say that your Columba's thoughts and feelings became yours, and perhaps vice versa?

JH: There was a mingling of sensibilities, for sure – I became so absorbed in Columba's world that I wasn't always certain whose voice was emerging. The first lines you quote are from an Old Irish poem, and the second ones emerged from my own quill, probably twitched by the spirit of Columba! He had a tremendous energy about him, and it came to me that the exhilaration you have when you're about to burst into song – that moment when you've made a decision to override your inhibitions and let rip – was typical of the way he lived his life. His energy also manifested itself when he was writing or copying in his scriptorium: the fingers of his writing hand were said to 'glow like five candles'. My writing fingers are usually lead-grey, I'm sorry to report, and swathed in fingerless gloves.

P McC: In the poem 'Defending the Poets' which is 'after the Irish', demonstrating the ancient wisdom of those very Irish, and the special place poetry had (still has) in their culture and in their hearts, there are the lines:

Colours blacken in the grave
  But poetry stays alive.

And the resounding crescendo at the end of the poem:

The grace of making poetry
  Is the greatest gift of time.

The sonnet here is broken up into quatrains. Does this symbolise the state of poetry today, splintered as it often is, without, if I dare say it, that vital 'grace' of language?

JH: This particular poem refers to the time when Columba attended a grand council in Ireland at which he successfully persuaded the local king not to expel the poets from his realm. So it's a sort of apologia for poetry, making a claim for its enduring nature. When I first came across the poem I was deeply moved by it – perhaps because during the first lockdown and also subsequently I felt the value of art, including poetry, was being questioned by myself, other practitioners, and also recipients. How can one justify spending a morning putting in a comma in a sonnet when hospitals are under siege (and then of course, as the story goes, taking out the comma in the afternoon)? In Ireland we were lucky to have strong advocates of the arts and voices asserting their crucial role in keeping society relatively sane. But I think all poets during the pandemic had to consider the worth of their vocation (which some do anyway on a daily basis). To discover Columba's confident defence of poetry was a brilliant moment. As for splitting the sonnet into quatrains, my lips are sealed!

P McC: Finally, is Columba's life and extraordinary world, full of miracles, a curio of a bygone age or does he have relevance in the modern world?

JH: Columba's *Life* (as told by Adomnán) opens up the mind and heart – as all tales of marvels do (which might be their best function) and reminds us of the central place of imagination in our lives. Also, in Irish culture Columba became the archetypal type of pilgrim known as the 'peregrinus'. Unlike later pilgrims who travelled with a set aim to a holy place such as Rome, the peregrini set out *without* a destination in mind – they allowed the wind to blow the sails of their boats wherever it would, believing that divine providence would guide them to the right place. In our micromanaged, Satnav worlds, this spirit of not-knowing where the journey might take us, but trusting implicitly in it, is like the most beautiful of all poems.

Gerard Smyth

The Haunted Radio

So many friends have gone to dwell in the haunted radio.
Some had no time for a last farewell,
some left in the dark thinking they'd be back.

One still had the smell of sweetened coffee on her breath,
a story half-read fell from her lap.
They have gone with their heartaches and worst mistakes

but also every gladness that they had.
Some with their love of Chopin and Bach,
the metaphors in Shakespeare's sonnets, Eliot's *Waste Land*.

Some left us when the fields were sinking deeper
into August grass, when a song we heard all summer
was dropping down the charts.

And then those others who blackened our festival of mirth,
who were lost to us in the chill
of the twelfth month, as if they discovered a vanishing trick.

Dublin Ode

There was the Liffy rolling downe the lea
                    – Edmund Spenser, *Irish Rivers*

I always loved the city, its detours and divisions.
The lights when darkness falls on it.
The clocks, the bells, steeples, domes –
whatever makes us look to its horizons.
I always loved the city.
The summer rain on statues,
street-names that take the strain of history.
Rush hour and the hour
when the empty streets are cleaned.
The monuments weathered into myth.
Swans in the canal looking radiant.
The river knows its way from source to sea,
runs past the riverside church:
Eve and Adam among Franciscan saints.
I always loved the city. It began
with father's Sunday walk from bridge to bridge
and the one time that he crossed
to see the other side. The lights along the river
make the river look like it's playing with fire.
A Liffey-wind comes with the tide
to sharpen the aroma of brewing yeast.
I always loved the city, its lanes that lovers walk.
The lanes that were the short way home
for those old wives who lived so long they saw
Lord Nelson toppled from his pinnacle.
We like it here beside the river,
gulls like feathered Buddhas perch on walls of stone,
men digging for leaks discover
earth-smelling bones
buried since a battle or a famine or a plague.

Leap Year

The day of no harm done,
the day to talk to no one.
The day of alarm-bells ringing,
like the sound of Armageddon.
The day to believe in luck
even as the March wind blows every door shut.
The day to join a conversation,
to be as honest as Augustine's *Confessions*.
The day when nothing rhymes,
to jot down thoughts, think twice.
The day we sit tight, feel the walls closing in.
The day to watch the sea waves
open the bottle of Burgundy wine.
The day that looks fine for a morning walk.
The day of losing precious time,
falling asleep in mid-afternoon.
The day the rain comes in through the roof.
The day the shades come down
to shut out the sun at high noon.
Then the day of so many weathers
we pass through wet sunshine.
The day for solemnity, the day for a joke;
the day to be in two minds and harbour both.
The day when nothing is certain
but so much happens the bottom falls out of it.
The day that is one more break with tradition,
the radio tuned to easy listening.
The day when the counting of days begins.
The day of mischance, blind chance, the last chance.
The day to gather the loose ends,
tidy up all that is scattered.

Counting to a Thousand

Anon

i

Like the time
you said (I hear how pleased and proud)
I can count to a thousand,
meaning a hundred. And the nanny
knowing what to do with joy
forced you to do it. Oh the tired
push through all that growth
of tedium, sense of less
and less achievement.
So the thousand
when at last – at last – it came in sight
was a noose, a terrible
let-down.
                    Is that how you felt
when his interest, kindness, his affection
turned to inordinate hunger, would not stop
putting you through his paces?

ii

For days afterwards
you felt you had been
opened like the carefully
stored grainsacks in the barn
and spilled across the yard.
You were empty forever and each
kernel bruising
in the muck and wet of light. You started
cramming them back in,
putting it all back –
any old how, just stuffing
the ruin back out of sight.

iii

The eyes of the kid
were yellow, unhinged. How must the world
look like through that slotted certainty?
You felt for the nubs of horn –
the skull; the brain
pulsing just under your fingers
but leagues from your grasp.
It butted against your hand –
a sickening purely
physical push.

iv

The house was large enough –
room after room, stretches
of slightly threadbare carpet, elegance
a little down on its luck.
Corridors tiptoed away
in quiet gloom, the hint
of must or mould.
You liked to watch the sunlight
silence an empty landing,
listen to the distant tinny
clatter from the kitchen, know yourself
quite separate. You liked to think
you could still be whoever you liked,
still dream, take flight.
The house was small enough
to vanish inside your head, pretend
night would never come, or not
yet, not yet
the goodnight kiss, the lurch
in your stomach as you woke
too quick, too hard and unable
to cry out because you were nothing,
tiny in his huge
will holding your tongue.

Perhaps he whispered (spare me
the suave cajole of his voice; but do you
sometimes still hear it at night?):
My special one. This is our
little secret. Let's keep it
just to ourselves, tell no one. No one
needs to know...
some cliché even then
you saw right through and yet
were swept up in the thought
of being real at last to someone, spun
into the conspiracy as his hand
pinning you plucked
a fruit you did not know you had
to give, admitted you to the pulse
thrilling at the place his hand
placed yours upon.

vi

Seemed to give you to yourself
as if he gave a gift: the sleight
of hand, the conman's trick
of robbing as he seems to give,
of draining as he seems to fill.
The thief kept circling back
to mouth the spring that made him quiver
alive with someone else's life, not caring
how fathoming the source his tongue
sealed up a deeper one.

vii

Moments when you nearly told
your mother? Maybe almost
opened your mouth to say, but at
the precipice of the moment felt
your mother knew already, was willing you not to lift
the mirror to her eyes and make

her know your face. Or felt
the chasm of connection,
vacuum space
you simply cannot get a word across.

viii

I see you waking suddenly at night
from a half-whole dream, almost
a child still – until
it all slides into place.
Somewhere in that silence
he's lying with your mother. A fox
makes some lonely, strangled sound
then stillness that's still worse.
For a moment you wish he'd come
so you could shout,
get all the lights turned on, the truth
stand naked in the house. But no,
night crams itself into your throat.
You turn your face back to the dark.

ix

It goes on. It's gone on too long, become
the ordinary tedium of the law
of his mouth stifling yours, his imperious
moustache, tobaccoey tweed, the cock
crowing inside you, demanding
and giving its dues.
And why mind after all?
This spasm called pleasure
is a small thing going on somewhere
while you're elsewhere: the lark
in the quail in the plover
in the goose in the swan.
And isn't he faintly ridiculous?
Heaving there blindly, not finding
the lodestone you keep lodging deeper because
the last thing, you've learned, that you'll give him
is the one thing he wants.

Stepping into drizzle, your mother
and you; and she fiddles
with an umbrella she lifts
over you both and puts
her arm comfortably in yours. And you think:
*This woman is my mother and loves me, but never
enough to have known.* And you think:
I will know my child better than this. And you think
of the small of his back, the bestial
hairs that repulse you and yet
the way you couldn't help touching, like she has,
that vulnerable place, with something like sorrow.
And you think:
perhaps you only wanted to connect
through him with her, to feel the places she,
to feel the things that she had felt.

xi

Lately, often, he's been giving
a quick slant look at you he thought
you didn't register.
Afraid of you?
He fusses around you like
a contraption he's invented:
checking the timing, adjusting a wingnut
with a tight smile, listening hard
to the hum or placing a hand
at a strategic place to calm
a rattle in the works.
Can he still keep the whole thing running smoothly?
What would he do if you started
to take on a life of your own?

xii

Jazz flaring from a gramophone.
You're smiling in the throng:
caught up in the release, one
sapling deep in the whole
fluttering forest and dancing
your body back into the spring
of itself, dancing
the world to a blur in which
everything is ringing, spun
easy, almost, with itself again.

xiii

He wants to be
the north your needle tremors on
the spine your breath is tethered to
the mind you think inside
the pole you grow around.
And he's holding on hard
to the harness of threads he's fixed
to your eyelids, mouth and breasts
your sex and tongue.
He's pulling but
the threats won't hold, first one
frays and then another however fast
he ties more on and tugs, and pins you down.
There's updraught under you; his strings
are fluttering loose and you
are clear of his gravity, now, looking back and seeing
a little man.

Linda Anderson

Vertigo

For some time now I've known this world and I are attached
only by a thread. It pretends I can see it

as it stretches its canopy of leaves and branches
and clouds over me. Then suddenly whisks it

away. A plane is banking steeply into the wind
and the fields turned around, copying the sky. Oh Alice,

what kind of truth are we falling away from? Everything
is galloping past in a blur, and all your sang-froid,

your air of control can't fix it. Detail is like
paint: it can peel, can be simply a mote or a fleck

on the preposterous coattails. It's already
too late to decide what's ground, what's ephemeral

in this headlong shimmering. Nothing is quite it. Hush.
Whisper. What kind of truth are we falling into?

Peter Carpenter

Grace's Field

'Whatever else, it was there before they built the by-pass.'
That's it, father, you lead me in with that voice lifting
itself from your page of notes, seventy years or more
after the fact, two years before you died, remembering
a year from your youth, my old lad – 1934.

Where was 'Grace's Field' then? And who would know?
Well then, it was all to do with lovely old horses
known as 'Vanners', the ones that pulled the carts
from the bakery to ensure the supply of bread to houses
as far afield as Worcester Park and Ewell Court.

Come Saturday afternoon, their working day done,
the horses seemed to know it was time for Grace's Field
and needed no great encouragement to get there. Harness
off, usual rub down, feed and a bucket of water. The ones
I remember the best were Mary, Ginger and Charlie.

In turn each had a halter put on, then about-turned
out of the yard, and the journey begun, me riding
alongside on a bike, with a yard of rein. High Street
negotiated, then, steady now, along the Cheam Road
past the Old Rookery and the medieval ash-pit

in 'The Elms', over the by-pass roundabout
until the turning before the Glyn Arms pub. Onto
a minor road, through the open lodge house gates
and a couple of hundred yards between an avenue
of trees. The big house with its high hedges is ahead

but we hang a right. And there it is, the magical
small field, almost oblong with a sharper end – there's
a stone water trough and the shelter of elms. Open
the gate, slip the reins, and off they go, galloping
and rolling, a brilliant day ahead. It's all gone

too fast – Monday, six a.m., time to go home. They know,
the three of them, and make for the end of the field.
The way to round them up comes with experience –
a long leather rein stretched out and now slow so slow
walk to the sharper corner – some minor resistance

but they know the drill and give in. Now back down
the Cheam Road into their stables on the High Street
then food, water, grooming and it's business as usual.
In your head you have the place, father, so it's time now
to lead you back, not yet a teenager, onto its two acre plot

where the rail and post-fence are still there along
with the old-fashioned hedge-row where blackbirds,
thrushes, hedge-sparrows, robins and wrens shimmer,
and high above, late into the summer evening, if you
really listen you can make out skylarks singing.

To my Physio

15th May, 2013

You took me by the arm
   and opened doors for me
expert with elbow and bum –
   you knew your stuff all right
from Art Deco to John
   Cooper Clarke ('Vacuum
Cleaner' the day you walked
   down the aisle) – and your name
will come back I'm sure along
   with the exact wording of your
one-liner about learning how
   to read from those lists – iron,
thiamin, riboflavin – you get on
the back of the Kelloggs'pack.

And we'll talk more I know
   about your favourite author, Homer –
and the voyage home from Troy,
   breaking the spell with Calypso.
Or your weakness for a glass or two
   of Malbec, its full-bodied texture,
(you should see the legs on it!). Maybe
   one Sunday when there's some slack,
I'll surprise you up on Level Three,
   sprightly as you like, but for now
forgive this breath-taking excuse,
   this old beggar shuffle from lift to
hall to automatic doors marked 'Exit'.

Shanta Acharya

Taste of Childhood

My itinerant tongue never forgot the taste of childhood –

the piquancy of pineapple, notes of peach and pear
in jackfruit, burst of honey in mango, melon and lychee,

the tangy zest of tamarind, sweet aftertaste of sour amla,
bitter neem and karela, the astringent bite of jamun

in the tree-climbing, limb-bruising days of hide-and-seek,
eating guava, papaya, sapetta. Digging for turmeric

in the sprawl of grandfather's grove facing the river,
bustling with wild life, including a family of otters –

islands quivering with a siege of herons practising
their moves while you spent orgasmic afternoons sucking

mango, munching raisin, almond and cashew,
waiting for a flash of kingfisher's indigo blue –

sipping nectar, sugarcane juice with salt and ginger,
swaying in a hammock from sturdy arms of nanny trees

when the world in your reach was for your pleasure,
ghar not mere bricks and mortar, but a state of belonging,

vilayat, the vast unknown out there, beckoning –
and you a sapling born to stay put, not travel hopefully.

Who would've thought years later the sparkling laughter
of pomegranates would reduce you to tears,

or the ceremony of cracking open the hard exterior
carry you home to the tenderness of kernel in the belly

of green coconuts and the soft, scented pulp
of ripe wood apples, tree sprung from the sweat

of a goddess, its sacred leaves offered in worship,
transport you to the inner sanctum of temples?

Like oranges, apples, bananas and grapes you make
a home of the world, holding your worlds together –

the place of your birth where all your efforts to escape
landed you in a place where all your attempts to belong

always pointed to a world elsewhere, leaving
you in-between, in a not-this-not-that state of being,

double helix of past and future wrapped round each other,
an afterwardsness, dancing to the music of the present.

This persistence of memory is no ordinary thing –
a lifeline like mother's milk, la dolce vita homecoming.

John Griffin

Skydance

He harries the air, a blade of wings
cutting currents into moves
he sashays to woo her – he rises
and glides, then pivots midflight,
the rudder of his tail turning on
the yaw and drag of his intent,
seducing the spaces she displaces,
an arrow shot from an invisible bow
at the eye of her indifference,
and now he freefalls, now hangs
as she soars, they almost collide,
except that he holds their torque
midsky and suspends it there,
where he extends weighted talons
and drops the payload he swaps
for her attentions, they slowly part,
as if some magnetic force refuses
to release them, as if dancing back
from this aerobatic glissade
that locked them in its pulse
and rhythm could finally free them
from the cadence of each other.

W.D. Jackson

Epiphany – Jack of Pentacles (The Space)

*This morning I am in a temper indolent and supremely careless... In this state ...
the fibres of the brain are relaxed in common with the rest of the body, and to such
a happy degree that pleasure has no show of enticement and pain no unbearable
frown...*

– Keats, *Letters (March 19, 1819)*

They lay calm-breathing on the bedded grass

– Ode to Psyche

You lie in the yellowish grass,
  Sunning your vivid skin;
Shadows approach, but pass;
  Your belly, hard and thin
  Beneath my fingers, rises
With every breath you take:
  Becoming used to surprises,
I want you so much I ache.

And want you until I'm afraid
  I'll *lose* what I can't possess.
Your brightness, also, will fade.
  Till even your folded dress –
  Your bra – your shoes – invite me,
Exposed to the sun on this hill,
  To clutch at what excites me,
To have – and hold – my fill...

But I hardly dare to move,
  You lie so entirely still,
Reading with faith – hope – love –
  A dead man's words, which will
  Always be with us now,
Bequeathing their timeless dream
  That our time-tied hearts might grow
To *be*, which merely seem...

Though we mostly prefer our lies:
    Pretending I'm *not* afraid,
My self-respect now tries
    With sun-drunk thoughts to evade
    Your past and mine – 'this world
Of Pains and troubles' – Death
And nightmare – this star-swirled
    Stagger from breath to breath.

– But as if a vertiginous hole
    Had gaped like a grave in me,
I suddenly reel and fall
    Reaching out helplessly
    From nowhere. De-construction
Of *then* and *now* – long years
    Of want and disaffection:
Failure – of even my fears

Of failure. Until this hillside
    Threatens to disappear:
Colourless, transparent, vacant,
    Far from either here
    Or elsewhere. Trapped in a dream,
In which I am wide awake,
    Stretched from extreme to extreme,
I feel myself starting to shake...

But my hands are still on your body;
    And now, as its blood pumps through
My relaxing panic, already
    My own blood starts to flow
    Again, till your inner quietness –
(A sort of loving trust) –
    Relieves my chest of its tightness,
Releases my breath – love – lust.

So breath by breath I return
  To my body, newly aware
Of your vivid limbs, which burn
  Bright and clear in the glare
  Your filtering skin receives:
You branch and flow like a tree;
  You have hair instead of leaves:
Your brightness is probing me.

A probing which seems to pull
  My searching hands apart:
One moves below your navel,
  The other beside your heart;
  And, breathing now together,
Our bellies rise and fall
  Till 'I' becomes the other,
Osmotic, each-in-all...

And again my limbs are branches
  Broader than death or birth,
And I know how a tree feels, standing
  Up to its waist in earth,
  While the current which flows between us
Is so clear and strong that we
  Are unable to stop our smiling
From setting each other free.

– The slower, heavier, longer
  This common life-stream grows,
The freer, stiller, stronger
  And less afraid each knows
  Their soul to be: each stands
Alone yet flows together;
  And still the current slows,
Till we flow away from each other

Into a blue-grey space
   So empty and so wide
It scarcely resembles a place,
   Though all that lives or has died
   Is eddying here, where life
And death swirl endlessly,
   Like peace at the heart of strife –
Or love between you and me.

Such love runs counter to fear;
   Its grateful spirit flows
Inwards and downwards to where
   The heart's still centre knows
   Nothingness cannot be:
It sees the way things are –
   And we are the way we see.
Love unfolds all we are.

And what if it should cease? –
   At the height of this ecstasy
My heart-beats rest in peace?
   I open my eyes and see
   A bluebottle land on the dull
Cloth which conceals your face,
   Whose skin conceals your skull:
We conceal an empty space.

Like grass between two stones
   Hair springs out of the gap
Between your thighs, whose bones
   Are not yet dry, whose sap
   Still rises. Though brightness dims,
And shapeliness loses its form,
   My limbs know now that your limbs
Are shapely, bright and warm.

And I don't know why or how,
　　But these words to you from me
Affirm that what's here now
　　Was once – has been – will be:
　　What state of mind adores?
I look but can find no fear.
　　Am I mine or am I yours?
Am I far away or here?

Note: 'Epiphany – Jack of Pentacles' is the concluding poem in an otherwise 3rd
person narrative sequence called *The House That Jack Built*. The jack – or page – of
pentacles (one of the four suits of Tarot cards) is described by A.E. Waite in *The Key
to the Tarot* (1910) as 'A youthful figure looking intently at the pentacle which hovers
over his raised hands.' In *From Ritual to Romance* Jesse Weston suggests that the
pentacle may be a female fertility symbol. It can, at any rate, be seen as representing
the five points of the body or the five senses. It was also long used in magic as a
sign for protection against evil spirits. The pentacle (or *'pentangel'*) is referred to in
Sir Gawayn and the Green Knight as 'the endeles knot' – presumably because the
interlacing lines of its five-pointed star (depicted in pure gold on Sir Gawayn's shield)
can be endlessly traced without lifting one's pen from the paper. The 'knot' is usually
self-contained, as its form implies. However, when it matches or merges with another,
a compound 'magic' is created in which the elements remain themselves and are also
more than themselves.

Greg Delanty

from *A New Field Guide to People*

Orca

Something's off about calling them *Killer* Whale,
or if not, what then should we call the likes of us
and many another killer with or without a tail?

Besides they are dolphins, inhabitants of Orcus.
And rightly so. For they are the ones who rule
the various ocean underworlds, discuss,

natter in dialect, protect and help each other, fool
and play about for hours (even with us);
love their mothers, their families, attend school;

learn languages, songs, echo scores; are various
as the gourd, plankton or the octopus,
always attending life's gala in their tuxedos,

a white-tie and tails affair, honored for their genius,
Nobel winners, bright as ourselves, the homunculus.

Parrot

Feather-brained, you kidding? This one is smarter
than I was at six—though, granted, I was a mite slow,
according to Brother Dermot, our headmaster,

raising the question mark of his cane, I, 'a holy show',
he parroting on about God, sin, hell and purgatory.
Can't spell 'abysmal'? Swish. Stand in the dunce row.

Can a parrot have dyslexia (a word nobody
knew back then)? We were just laggards, lay-
abouts, wasters, slackers, sloths, plain lazy.

Not so, the persistent parrot; consider Alex say:
he could spell, form proper sentences (went to
Harvard even). Asked what colour he was: 'I'm gray.'

Now we are wiping out this colourful, chatty kind too.
His last words: 'Be good. See you tomorrow? Love you.'

Diana Cant

Birdman

I make you bird:
you arrive in different guises,
each bright-billed and wind-ruffled –

a feathered native, dark and querulous,
a rook, a raven; or something more exotic
flying in from steamy rainforest –

my birdman lover,
my bird of paradise,
my homespun blackbird.

Today I hold your fledgling head
eggshell-fragile and baby-bald,
sun-vulnerable

your bones shiver
as they feel their strength return,
migration on their mind –

it is summer
and you are recovering:
stay.

Caroline Maldonado

Eleanor Hooker: *Of ochre and ash* (Dedalus Press, 2021)
Annemarie Ní Churreáin: *The Poison Glen* (Gallery Press, 2021)

Reading Eleanor Hooker's collection feels like entering a novel made up of surreal, complex narratives. Everything is itself and something *other*, there are many selves, doppelgangers and the pages are populated by myths, family memories and histories. Yet the narrative is not sequential, it lives in the images that take on shifting resonances as they echo back and forth throughout the book and this review will attempt to give a sense of their effect as a structure underpinning the whole.

Hooker lives in rural County Tipperary overlooking a lake and is a helm for the Royal National Lifeboat Institution. She has also worked as an intensive care nurse. Both are practical life-saving occupations bringing her into close proximity with death and the liminary. Ghosts of the past haunt the collection and many poems suggest the poet's attempt to come to terms with them. The ash in the title is associated with death but another reference may be to the tree. The ash tree as well as the rowan and the quicken tree that also feature in the collection, all play a role in Celtic mythology, representing communication with the spirit world, rebirth and woman's discovery of the self.

Clay is one of the recurring images. The ochre in the title is a clay earth with a red pigment, associated with life blood. In the context of the poem from where the title is drawn the phrase relates to grasslands, a place of nurture for the poet, but it carries a bloody history:

> here grasslands smell of ochre
> and ash, of scorched heartlands'
> ('When you dream of the Dead')

Elsewhere clay suggests our earth-bound nature and in 'Eating the Earth' it becomes a healing substance. The first three stanzas of this poem are located in the poet's own beloved landscape, where she is digging potatoes. This inevitably recalls Heaney's 'Digging' but the poem soon follows its own path. Drawing on her own experience as a nurse, in the second poignant section of the poem she describes a man brought into hospital by his elderly sister. Like many old men living alone in the countryside he has tried to kill himself, with weed-killer. 'His sister knew enough to make him eat earth' to counter the effects of the poison and the nurse coaxes 'him to eat/the

Fuller's Earth [a kind of clay] I've prepared' until finally 'He sleeps/beneath the earth, a clay blanket over his bleached bones'. In the final section a rock in the ground seizes the poet by her wrist: 'makes me one of its secrets, roots me/to the vernacular of the earth on whose lie my life depends'.

The potatoes still echo in the reader's mind two poems later in 'Exquisite Corpse'. After its first harmless-sounding line, 'An ordinary hungry family', it develops into a bitter poem referring to, without naming, the Irish Famine and 'Ms Britain's/new young face, that cost them the earth'.

Another recurrent metaphor is that of snow. In the first poem of the collection its relationship to death is established:

> As though on a cloud, he lay on the snow, newly dead –
> feather and frame round blown glass. It felt transgressive
> to spread his wing, to inspect. Inside my ribcage, my ruby-throated
> hummingbird turns the key; fearful I will fall through my song.
>
> ('Redwing')

Later, 'A Landscape Forfeited to Snow', a poem whose staccato sentences and imperative tense heightens its sense of urgency, opens with a clinical operation opening a woman's body, and in 'Ossuary', a moving poem about a still birth: 'Your baby kicks the snowfall dusting/the landscape inside you'. In both these poems the snow is internal, opening to another potential world.

A prominent theme in the collection is that of the violence suffered by women. The loss of another baby is the subject of 'Delivery', in which a woman is 'raped into motherhood' and deprived of her child as one of the women incarcerated in the Irish Magdalene Laundries. In 'Tamponade' a surgeon attempts unsuccessfully to remove a blood clot from the fifth rib of an eight year old girl. The verse below, together with the reference to blood and rib, echo the first poem in the collection about the 'ruby-throated' redwing, reinforcing our close connection to the natural as well as the spirit world:

> You do not pray:
> you speak homing words
> to her bird-spirit,
> that hovers, heartsore.

Hooker writes in a rhythmic, musical free verse, often structured into stanzas of equal lines, in a voice that ranges between violence and despair and a delicate lyricism. Occasionally she uses inventive devices, such as the visual effect of columns and erasure, or a cryptic crossword ('My Mother as a Cryptic Crossword') or a formal Q&A ('Interview with Honeybee as Poet') which add to the unsettling sense of disturbance in the collection, represented elsewhere by water, tossing boats and even a room that lists. Her sources are various: Celtic myths, the Bible, Dante's 'Divine Comedy', Pullman's 'His Dark Materials'and a Josh McCrae song among others. The ghosts of earlier writers appear. Heaney has been mentioned, another is Yeats hovering behind 'From my Hazel Wood' a lyrical poem in which Hooker rows across the lake 'to see my home from the other side'. Many poems have epigraphs to writers and the literary references provide an extra dimension to this already multi-dimensional, imaginative work in which darkness is bravely explored but is balanced by the life-affirming power of the natural world, and by the final poem 'Lifeboat':

no longer will we fear the fog's fret, that mimes
the snow-blind clime inside our eyes, now, when we leave the quay,
four up, our *Jean Spier* will signal those in peril, or in strife.
that we her volunteers may do our work – carry home, save a life.

*

Annemarie Ní Churreáin leaves no doubt as to her intention and theme in this, her second collection after her debut, 'Bloodroot' (Doire Press, 2017). It is a collection driven by its subject matter, the hidden story of missing children stolen from their mothers, and of the Irish church and state-run institutions which held them in conditions of physical and mental torture, often to death, from the1700s to the mid-1800s. Myth is woven with personal and communal testimonies as a way of approaching this difficult, painful material, with a half page introduction setting out the myth and the title reference. There is a place in North West Donegal known as 'The Poisoned Glen' associated with the evil-eyed King Balor who imprisoned his daughter Eithne in an island tower and tried to drown her infants for fear of the prophecy of his own death, only finally to be killed by his own exiled grandson. The voices in the collection include those of Eithne and Eithne's mother, as well as of other abandoned, bereaved and grieving women.

In the poem 'The Screaming Room' Ní Churreáin visits a hut once put out on a lawn for women who, in pain from their labour, screamed too loudly. There she states her personal interest: 'I come from women who found themselves/in trouble, who turned to their pale reflections/and asked, *What can I do? What can I do?*' Her own paternal grandmother was sent to the Castlepollard Mother and Baby Home where she was forced to relinquish her child to adoption. The child was the poet's father and one of the themes she traces is that of the impact of history on the present day and the need to confront it 'what cannot be written is rising up/through the cracks' ('Southistle') Her mother adopted many foster children and the experiences of her foster-siblings also informed her anger and her search for knowledge, leading into the research detailed in the back pages of the book.

Questions are a feature of many of the poems, either personal, as in the quote above, or addressed to history. There are existential questions about evil, suffering, survival and others relating to restorative justice; all are rooted in the events themselves. The main voice is that of the story-teller and the urgency is that of drama – rhetorical devices such as questions (or alternatively accusations) contribute to the effect. The poems are grounded in realistic detail despite their mythical and dream-like quality and they are dramatic while avoiding melodrama. In 'A Sentence' the reader is drawn in with the physical particular of sound but the emotion rises until the last sentence which cuts away with an almost ironic tone:

At first it was like waking up underwater.
    She could hear the muffled din of a neighbour

dragging a wheelie bin across the concrete yard.
    She wanted to run up to the cold, thin surface

of her old life yelling *My son, my son*. Even so,
    it was no time for theatrics.

('A Sentence')

Often Ní Churreáin turns to communal forms of language, taken from religion and folklore and listed in the titles of many poems: 'Creed', 'Baptism', 'Catechism of a Boy's Reform School', 'A Handmaid's Incantation against Silence', 'A Charm to protect a Girlchild', 'A Charm to Call a Cow into your Dreams' 'Sunday Sermon' and the final one 'A Blessing of the Boats by the Village Mothers'. How the content changes within that recognised form can be seen in the following poem, where the figure of resurrection has become a terrible parody. Other characteristics of her writing are also caught in this section, the visceral emotional quality, the sensory detail, strong imagery, musicality and rhythm.

Weeping, The Child escaped out through a crack
in the wall, was brought back in again, split
open at the hip and stitched up without pill or balm.
The Child descended into a dreamless state,
and on the third day rose from the dormitory bed –
hungry, swollen, wet to the skin.
The Child ascended the stairwell,
and on the third day rose from the dormitory bed –
hungry swollen, wet to the skin.
The Child ascended the stair well,
and on the first floor curled up, like a doll torn apart
by an angry dog, at the right hand of The Sister.'

('Creed')

A powerful longer poem, a poetic sequence of ten sections, 'The Foundling Crib', bears an epigraph from Eavan Boland from 'Child of our Time'. According to the notes, the poem references the histories attached to what was The Foundling Hospital, an institution passed through by as many as 200,000 children. The couplets start by describing the hunger, cold and starvation on the streets of Dublin but the poem's focus is on the story of Bridget Kearney who was parted from her baby girl there. Ní Churreáin establishes her own human responsibility in the fifth section: '*I am not She. I am mother./She is not forgotten. She is my daughter*'. With the omission of the definite article before 'mother', the lines are lifted to a mythical or at least communal level. And in the ninth section is a remarkable expression of compassion using anaphora to attract our human empathy directly:

Pity the foundlings in the wake of Arbella,
gathered at a rare fire, cupped hands begging the heat.

Pity their uplit cheekbones
like the death petals of a cursed buttercup.

Pity their fingers, swollen and stiff.
Pity their skins needles with poisons to trial medicines.

('The Foundling Crib')

Unusually, in this case Bridget returned with 'a foundling price in her pocket, a demand on her lips' to bring her little girl home with her.

'A Blessing of the Boats by the Village Mothers', the final poem in 'The Poison Glen', commissioned by the Fanad Lighthouse, County Donegal, transforms images from fishing superstition and folklore into a blessing for those lost at sea and the boats as they put out. The last line 'We keep the light for safe return' ends the collection with some hope as Ní Churreáin brings the voices of hidden women and their children out into the open, a passionate step towards restorative justice in the form of poetry.

Elizabeth Barton

Living Dark: New Poetry

Tess Jolly: *Breakfast at the Origami Café* (Blue Diode Press, 2020)
Jane Lovell: *The God of Lost Ways* (Indigo Dreams Publishing, 2020)
Matthew Barton: *Dusk* (Shoestring Press, 2021)
Gill Learner: *Change* (Two Rivers Press 2021)
Gill McEvoy: *Are You Listening?* (The Hedgehog Poetry Press, 2021)

We all have our ways of coping with loss. The poets in these collections look outwards towards the needs of others and journey inwards, deep into the psyche, where painful experiences are transformed by the power of the imagination.

Nothing is quite what it seems in Tess Jolly's dazzling and disorienting first collection, *Breakfast at the Origami Café*. She trespasses on territory where few poets dare to venture, confronting family trauma and the violent inheritance we may unwittingly pass on to our children. There is a stifling atmosphere of secrecy, '…of stories not yours to tell that leave their scars on the dream/landscape…' The poem of the collection's title shifts from the reassuring familiarity of 'coffee and pastries' to the surreal image of a girl folding herself '…smaller/and smaller until there is nowhere left to go'. In 'Gaps', lines slide down the page like the mysterious 'we' who make themselves like insects, '…small enough/to crawl through the socket/of this dead gull's eye…'. Insects scuttle in and out of this collection – woodlice, spiders, wasps – their need to hide, and their propensity for both spinning and stinging, mirroring the human world.

This bold opening sequence is followed by tender poems set in The Lake District about the poet's father who has been diagnosed with an illness. In this delicate metaphor in 'Cairn', '…your skin drapes/round your bones in ruffles and folds/stitched with your vein's brocade…', it is as though he too is disappearing. There is a fascination with skin, paper and cloth – materials which are all too easy to tear or pierce. The poems are also haunted by the mother/grandmother archetype associated with secrecy and the spinning of human fate. We meet the poet's grandmother in the third sequence of poems and it is here that we discover the origin of some of Jolly's fears, such as her terror of passing on 'a knowledge of violence' to her children. These prose poems, rich, strange and skilfully narrated, are the dark heart of the collection. After their spellbinding intensity, the last section feels a little less compelling, although poems such as 'Dating Scan' are unbearably poignant. Overall, this is an extraordinary debut collection.

*

Equally dark and unflinching is 'The God of Lost Ways' by Jane Lovell. The collection comes highly recommended by two of our finest nature writers, Mark Cocker and Miriam Darlington. The opening poem, of the same title, captivates the reader with its portrayal of a mysterious, 'mercurial' god. He embodies both the chaotic, destructive aspects of nature and its healing powers: 'He unfurls…/linnets and pipits to stitch paths/across your discarded landscapes'. The poem seems to offer hope that, although our relationship with the natural world is broken, we only need to follow the god's signs – a 'jay's feather in your hand', a 'greenlip marble' – to find our way back. Lovell has a musical ear and her use of language is highly original. She reclaims words from dialect, such as 'scrattle', giving her poetry a primeval, earthy texture. Her writing can be appreciated with both the eye and the ear, as in this description of the starling, with its 'slinted claw/and oilbead plumage, its gloss-speckle and lustre//crisp-folded on the cusp of winter'.

Lovell writes with a remarkable quality of attention and an intimate knowledge of the landscape. She has that rare ability to see through a wild creature's eyes, as in 'On Rye Hill' – terrain she knows well from her role as Rye Harbour Nature Reserve's former Writer-in-Residence. She entices the reader by giving clues regarding the speakers' identity, '…blunt claws scuffing root and soil/from earthy chambers…', '…we scatter from the scent of fox…', whilst never naming the creatures explicitly, lending them an air of mystery. The theme of mortality permeates this collection but while these animals live amongst the bones of the dead, Lovell is depicting a world in which earth, sea and sky are heaving with life. She reimagines the world through their senses, describing how they measure time by 'the creep of ivy' and 'the tilting of the light'. In 'I am a wren', her desire to become a wild creature is almost fulfilled: '…built of the thinnest bone,/I am almost flying.' These are poems to relish, enlivening the senses and reawakening the reader's sense of wonder.

*

Mortality weighs heavily in the other three collections, all of which centre on the loss of a partner. Following the death of his wife, Matthew Barton takes the reader on an unsettling journey through the different stages of grief in 'Dusk'. These are deeply personal, emotionally powerful poems, all the more striking for being unassuming and spare. Like Jolly's collection, the poems often begin in a familiar world, only to startle you with their strange insights, like the barn owl that suddenly appears in the opening poem of same title: 'It was death/bearing the world alive/through living dark.' There are disturbing images, as in 'Kittens': '...the grief that keeps//coming up for air however much/you hold it down and wait for it to stop.' This haunting metaphor evokes both the speaker's grief and his boyhood guilt at disposing of the drowned kittens' bodies when asked to do so by an adult.

Barton strives, above all, for truth and does not shy away from his ambivalent feelings towards his wife. In 'It Was Only The Wind', he captures the chaotic aspect of their relationship in the image of the broken window: '...I let them lie://the mess of splinters, bits of fallen sky.' Here, the end rhymes hint at a longing for resolution. In 'Sabre Wasp', he refers again to the 'terrible battles' he and his wife fought but acknowledges that, like the predatory insect he is observing, she was '...still/vulnerable, beautiful.' This raw and moving opening sequence gives way to more contemplative poems, such as 'Walking', in which the speaker yearns to be 'alive to the earth' again. Barton understands the limitations of language and when his mother suffers a stroke, losing her speech, it seems to stir a welling up of love and compassion. Ironically, it is this 'release' from words that gives mother and son access to a more direct form of communication, the language of touch, as he describes poignantly in 'Struggle': '...you reach for my hand/not in need but in love.' Words, as he states in 'Stroke', '...no longer get in the way.'

*

While Barton shines a forensic light on the nature of grief, Gill Learner, in her third collection, 'Change', addresses both personal loss and broader issues, including conflict and the environment. The title is stark but her poems seem to be motivated by a deep longing for change, for a society which acknowledges our shared humanity. Her love of the arts is reflected in her poems about the tumultuous lives of writers, artists and musicians. Her sequence of ekphrastic poems is impressive, especially her fantasy about swimming with one of Anthony Gormley's barnacled sculptures on Crosby Beach: 'We'll.../freestyle our way past Ynys Mon/into the starry darkness of the Irish Sea.' This is followed by moving poems about her husband's sudden death. The first of these, 'How it was', is all the more devastating for being understated and restrained. The lines are long and leisurely, giving the reader a false sense that the morning rituals she describes will go on for ever: 'Coffee brewed,//I picked up the paper from the mat, made for the sun-room…' The contrast in the abrupt last line, 'you'd gone', is harsh, the empty space echoing the speaker's shock and disbelief. This is followed by 'Strange beast' in which, like Barton's 'Kittens', grief is personified, resurfacing when we least expect it: 'Although I learned to lock it in the house,/at times it would escape, stalk me, grab me by the throat…'

Despite her personal grief which she conveys so vividly, Learner remains fully engaged with the world. She is a poet with a strong social conscience and some of her most passionate poems are about the dispossessed. It is as if, when writing about the suffering of others, she overcomes her own reticence, creating powerful, unsettling poems. In 'Ex', about a wounded soldier, she captures the hell of life on the streets with surreal and disturbing images: 'At night, among the city's strays, he swears/widows have stuffed nettles in his sleeping-bag, mothers/scrape nails across his skin…' Provocatively, in the last verse she switches from using the pronoun 'they' to 'you': 'You may well pass him, cross-legged on his sleeping bag,/wheezing music…' These are thought-provoking poems, generous in their compassion.

*

'Are You Listening' by Gill McEvoy takes the reader by surprise, its sombre cover barely hinting at the richness and colour within it. It explores the poet's complicated grief for her husband which, as she warns from the beginning, '…grew more intense with the passing of time.' This knowledge creates tension, as the reader anticipates a second wave of grief more terrible than the first. We are held in suspense until the very last line, as the speaker vacillates between feelings of exasperation and love. McEvoy writes with refreshing honesty, refusing to take solace in hackneyed proverbs, as in 'Old Wounds': '*Time*, they say, *will heal*. I say no:/wounds and bruises deepen.' In 'The Wayward Button', in which she describes burning her husband's coat on Bonfire Night, she is candid about the unrelenting demands of caring for an ill spouse whilst raising a family. With brutal frankness, she writes, 'God knows that coat was you,/stubborn in the way it wouldn't burn…', only to succumb to tenderness when she discovers a button has survived the flames.

Many of the poems are daring in their spareness and have an imagistic feel. One of the most poignant of these is 'They Say The Last Colour We See Is Blue', in which the speaker imagines what her husband might have seen on his deathbed: '…purple-blue of Irish hills,//…Or the perfect blue/ of the small forget-me-not…' The poem is a series of questions, reaching out yearningly into white space, giving it a prayer-like quality. McEvoy's diction is simple but her writing is never prosaic. She has a gift for the visual and, as in Sylvia Plath's poetry, colours are important symbols, signalling emotions and themes. Gradually, the mood of the poems shifts from the blue of mourning and spirituality towards the green of hope and rebirth. There are poems about apples, about the green light that envelops her new home, about her renewed love for her husband: 'Green, like your eyes/that glinted a sea-change/whenever a story rose in your mind.' There is a rich interweaving of imagery towards the end of the collection, increasing the emotional intensity of the writing and conveying the speaker's powerful sense of loss:

The pockets of my heart are filled
with holes, not stars, the bright apples
always out of reach.

Caroline Maldonado

Chris Beckett: *Tenderfoot* (Carcanet, 2020)

Chris Beckett's *Tenderfoot* follows his two other Carcanet publications, the much praised *Ethiopia Boy* (2013) and *Songs we Learn from Trees* (2020), an anthology of Ethiopian Amharic poetry edited and translated with Alemu Tebeje. Beckett grew up in the 1960s and in the preface to his first collection tells how only after he'd started translating Amharic poems did 'the real voice of my boyhood come spilling out'. It is the physical presence of that 'voice' that is so enticing in both collections and the richness of imagery, leaping syntax, humour and sensuality. The first book was a collection of 'praise shouts' whereas *Tenderfoot* (a newcomer or novice, especially a person unaccustomed to hardship (OED)) is more a 'coming of age' collection, exploring the love of place and relationships with their contradictions, as a white boy in an African country. The form of many of these poems continues to borrow from Amharic poetry, including praise shouts, and space on the page is used inventively.

Tenderfoot also approaches the unmentionable: Hunger. One poem 'Malnourished' provides the blunt statistics 'one in four children, stunted/ one in ten/hanging by a thread/one in twenty, dead'. The second poem in the collection is 'for Abebe, i.m.' a beloved friend who lived and died in *Ethiopia Boy*. Beckett addresses him here after seeing a 'red-eyed roadside boy/furiously begging to be fed':

> do any of us really understand, Abebe
> how finger close a boy can be
> and still have nothing   nothing
> of the world's good bread?
>
> ('Good Bread')

Hunger can express itself in many ways, including physical, emotional and spiritual. Another 'unmentionable' in many societies is still homosexuality and Beckett's awareness of his own desires is beautifully explored in this poem:

What is a storm if not weeping?
   and the boy
washing himself in the storm
   with rough hands
and soap   is he not a slim trunk of water
   attracting thirsty looks from the track?
                      ('Elegy for a thunderstorm')

And in these lovely first lines:

Some walk into a sunbeam
and their heads catch fire
   ("When I was ten, I started watching men')

There's much more to be said about the imaginative, linguistic and emotional energy of Beckett's writing than can be covered in a brief review. Enough to say here that I read *Tenderfoot* straight through from start to finish and felt nourished by it.

Robert Selby

Will Stone: *The Slowing Ride* (Shearsman)

That ardent advocate of European unification, Stefan Zweig, viewed Continental civilisation as a Tower of Babel that could reach unlimited heights should its many tribes learn to live beyond 'the isolation of their languages' and work together. In fact, Zweig, writing in 1916, propounded the notion that the Great War was man's punishment by an insecure God for the Tower's second rise (after the first depicted in the Book of Genesis), a rise that reached its apogee with the liberal Hapsburg realm of which Zweig, born in Vienna in 1881, was a product. But even at this darkest hour of industrialised slaughter on the Somme and in Galicia, Zweig believed that some vestige of their 'communal youth' remained in the peoples of Europe and that poets would again translate 'the words of their brothers into their own languages'.

Another world inferno and, it's fair to say, some fairly mixed post-war decades later, Zweig's translator into English, Will Stone, is another vestigial poet of pan-Europeanism in a time of fracture. Habitually crossing from his Suffolk home on Europe's edge deep into its cultural heartlands, he has translated into English a growing number of the Continent's literary nobility – de Nerval, Verhaeren, Rodenbach, Rilke, Roth, Trakl, and Zweig – while writing his own ferocious, densely-packed, metaphor-rich verse. Ferocious, for Stone lacks Zweig's body armour of naivety – he is wholly unillusioned and clear-eyed in his elegies for what he believes has expired or is expiring: frontier-transcending intelligence, embodied by great works of art, music, literature and architecture, as well as their creators. His *oeuvre* is less melancholic than simmering with anger as the skies close in.

Philistinism, materialism and the ersatz are in Stone's cross-hairs and he is unafraid to let his exasperation at what he sees as their rise draw him into the outskirts of misanthropy, as when, in the opening poem of his first collection, *Glaciation* (Salt, 2008), today's generation is imagined playing on 'unaware that plans are in the final stages / for its obliteration', which will end 'all the effluent that darkens the earth / from the outflow of their shadow'. As the poem's title 'Restoration' suggests, humanity's end merely means a fresh start for everything else. This foreshadowing of apocalypse is ever-present, coals to the remorseless Stone engine, but the end times occasionally advance out into the light to make themselves known, as in 'Exodus' where the motley crew of humanity's last survivors ('a gaggle of jaded porn stars / smoking crack and, unrecognised, / a media baron devouring his own face') collect on a beach, the sea blocking further flight. There comes no salvation, no parting of the waves to allow a crossing, and 'smothering their still struggling dreams / they sink down one by one / onto the point of the sun's keen lance'. Stone's lack of equivocation is buttressed by his poetry's rejection of a modish conversational diction for a muscular, punchy one (note, for example, the monosyllabic last two lines of the preceding quote) in which every word is doing heavy lifting. The result is a commanding intensity now rare in British poetry: the shrug is anathema to Stone and he is not bashful with the platform the page gives him.

That said, increasingly with proceeding collections – his second *Drawing in Ash* (Salt, 2011) and then most of all with his third, *The Sleepwalkers* (Shearsman, 2016) – gorgeous lyrical lines pierce the muscularity: a meadow is an 'ante-room / to the shadow emporium'; in the Valois 'on the lake's slender arm, dragonflies / repair the nets of surface shadow'; a sand timer 'bows to the thirst / of the sand to build its glitter dune'; discarded belongings in an extermination camp are 'lost / bobbing in the jaundiced foam / of history's exhausted wave'. This last example is taken from a sequence that obliquely addresses the Holocaust, an event which, he explains in a note appended to his latest collection, *The Slowing Ride* (Shearsman, 2020), has transfixed Stone since he was a schoolboy, when reading *The Final Journey* by Gudrun Pausewang one afternoon in the school library triggered 'a lifetime's ultimately futile search to somehow gain mental purchase on the most industrially realized genocidal event in human history'. Here we glimpse the adolescent, 1970s Stone already looking to Europe enquiringly, as a cradle both of high art and the basest of crimes – and the death camps inevitably haunt his poetry. The Holocaust stands as the supreme warning against philistinism and – Stone argues in his introduction to his translations of some of Zweig's prose, *Messages from a Lost World* (Pushkin, 2017) – more specifically nationalism, which is 'the sworn enemy of civilisation, whether past, present or future'. Channelling Zweig, Stone's poetry portrays humanity at a tipping point, as the eponymous sleepwalkers, moving towards destruction – environmental, pestilential, genocidal: 'For every evil, they blame each other, / on how to go forwards or back / they cannot agree, or decisively act.' But, as we have seen, Stone in his pessimism goes a step further than Zweig: the tipping point is in fact already behind us, and the 'storm waves are below the last house, / tireless, itching for the cornerstone':

All are inside, millions to a room
they fire flares, write pressing articles,
but for Europe, our beautiful bone yard,
the last ship of culture rich centuries
has passed on.

> ('What once was hidden will now appear', *The Sleepwalkers*)

Published in October last year, *The Slowing Ride* – with its further talk of 'our shattering impermanence' – brought no relief for the locked-down reader awaiting good news. The prospect of a dystopian Bio Security State arising as a consequence of Covid-19 lends greater resonance to lines penned in response to the 2019 Tory party conference: 'The governing hand finally fails, / becomes a sideways scooping palm'. Stone builds on his portrait portfolio of writers and artists *in extremis*, with Goya (a stroke), Marguerite Bervoets (the Gestapo guillotine) and Paul Celan (suicide) all succumbing this time, the extinguishing of their flames symbolic of a wider termination of truth amid the barbarism. 'Ice' is referred to repeatedly in the opening poems as civilisation's fires are kicked out; enlightenment is locked up, tantalisingly near beyond the translucent but impenetrable, recalling the drowning of German writer Georg Heym on the frozen river Havel, a former subject of Stone's. Parisian artist Charles Meryon's incarceration in the Charenton lunatic asylum is here vividly revisited ('the linen was fresh and neatly piled, / horribly aligned the brush and comb') following an earlier go in *Drawing in Ash*. Stone's lament for the touristifaction of cultural sites continues in 'Vanished Spirit of Bruges' and 'The Garden of Silence', the latter poem, about a Piedmont monastery where convent sisters sequester themselves from day-trippers, also building on a discernible reverence for the religious – or at least spiritual – sanctum in Stone's poetry. (The spiritual realm, after all, can be father to the artistic and the contemplative missions of both have a similar air of fragility and futility in our cacophonous late modernity.) Some of the pleasing results of this recall R.S. Thomas without the jazzy enjambment, such as the 'Winter Light' on the cathedral angels in *Glaciation*:

The beautiful gift of their decay.
Nailed there, saturated with prayer,
they bless the terrified birds outside
losing strength in the black hedges.

> ('Winter Light', *Glaciation*)

Like the 'warm rain' of prayer in Thomas's 'The Belfry', which miraculously cuts through the cold countenance of the poet and his church

– bringing 'the sun and afterwards the flowers / on the raw graves and throbbing of bells' – so Stone's poem 'Sleepwalkers II', in *The Sleepwalkers,* is antidote to the first instalment of that name and Stone's otherwise firm incredulousness. An 'un-sacred child', 'resisting the ruffed angelic', steps forward from the choir in Burgundy's Vézelay Abbey, begins a solo 'and the voice / simply stepped out from his soul', reversing – if only fleetingly – Stone's certainty of 'another century / of darkness'. The calibre of this dazzling, revelatory poem is emblematic of *The Sleepwalkers* as a whole; a masterful collection that ought to be better known.

The *Slowing Ride* perhaps fails to reach such heights quite so consistently, but further shores-up an important, already substantial and happily still accumulating vision. Many of its stronger pieces read like ripples still emanating out from its powerful predecessor. For example, 'The Last Pilot', a tribute to the last living Battle of Britain pilot, is a moving complement to *The Sleepwalkers'* 'Where the Airman Are' – a lump-in-the-throat elegy for a Lancaster bomber crew buried in a Brussels cemetery – as well as the important 'Departure of the Loved Ones', about Stone's parents and their generation receding 'in a chaos / of technology and systems, of guards / and glass and people who do not know'. In the face of this singular generation 'darkness shrank back', if only for a while, and their moving into history leaves us somehow adrift, unable to agree on how to go forwards, or back, the Tower of Babel in disrepair, the workers having long lost their way.

John Bourke

Which *ciao* will it be?

Greg Delanty: *No More Time* (Louisiana State University press, 2020)

In 1932, the American poet William Carlos Williams pronounced –

> 'Don't write sonnets. The line is dead, unsuited to the language.
> Everything that can ever be said from now until doomsday in the
> sonnet form has been better said in twelfth-century Italian'.
> > (*Selected letters* p134: ed, John C. Thirlwall, 1984)

More than thirty years later a fellow American poet, John Berryman, was to win the Pulitzer prize for Poetry with his ground-breaking *Dream Songs* which stood, predominantly, as an extended love poem outside the strict sonnet form. Berryman was no stranger to pronouncements of his own, but in his *Sonnets* (published in 1967 and written some twenty years before *Dream Songs*) we find an American voice that blends mid-twentieth century slang with Elizabethan euphony in the sonnet form.

In *No More Time*, Greg Delanty does something similar with his native Cork voice through the medium of late medieval/early Renaissance terza rima, the greatest example of the latter being Dante Aligheri's *Divine Comedy* (published 1320). Just as Dante's great work journeys through Hell, Purgatory and Paradise, Delanty, in his latest volume, inhabits a triptych of fear in that we have run out of time for preserving our mother-planet –

> She may need the kiss
> of life. She'll recover for sure, only without
> us maybe.
> > ('One More Time')

One of Berryman's pronouncements was 'We must travel in the direction of our fear'. Delanty's fears for the future form the bedrock of this ambitious poetic endeavour –

> Her ageing body is becoming a living shell,
> *Terra Mater*, the erasing of cell after cell.
> > (Untitled, 'Breaking News')

The twenty-six sonnets (following an alphabetical order of sequence and known as *diaspora* sonnets) that account for Parts 1 and 3, cryptically titled *A field Guide to People,* echoes the poet's Prefatory Note where he says 'Consider what follows as writing by an animal'. The middle section, titled *Breaking News*, presents a snapshot of our contemporary status quo of ignorance, indifference, apathy and arrogance across twenty-five poems where the sonnet and terza rima (apart from nine poems) are eschewed for more free-standing forms. The possible pun on 'breaking' here would not be out of place even if there is understated irony in the use of 'news' in relation to the calamity that is about to befall us if humankind's mistreatment of climate and planet continue unchecked. The entire collection is previewed and concluded, respectively, with *Loosestrife* as a 'purple plague' and the wonderfully enigmatic 'We're done.' of *Envoy: Zayante* acting like bookends on the mantelpiece of ecological disaster.

The only other sequence of the *diaspora* sonnets is Percy Bysshe Shelley's 'Ode to the West Wind', but critics feel that he couldn't manage the form. There are individual versions of this type of sonnet, such as Robert Frost's 'Acquainted with the Night'. (Indeed, Frost lived the last twenty years of his life in Vermont – just south of Burlington, where Delanty has lived since 1986).

Just as Dante employs Virgil and Beatrice as his *poetic enablers*, and as does (often perversely) Berryman employ his alter ego, Henry, Delanty employs *Gaia* (earth-mother) as his travel guide –

The angle of her head on the pane reminds me

Of the tilt of the earth. Bingo,
I knew she looked familiar: Gaia, leaning on the window.
('The Red Eye')

And when he digs out lowly earthworms he calls –

Build them a shrine.
May these lowly laborers of Gaia

multiply, flourish, never decline,
stick with worm love, position 69.
('Earthworm')

Name checked or not, Gaia's presence is all-pervading, so much so that the depth of Delanty's ideological environmentalism prevents *No More*

Time from being exclusively 'Gregorian cant and rant' (from *Envoy* that concludes the entire sequence) or a political treatise. But not all creatures under Gaia's motherly arm fall neatly into the 'inventory' of being elected as being

> denizens of a kind of *Paradiso*.
> But consider the likes of a particular wasp,
> The tarantula hawk, straight out of the *Inferno*.

whose

> larva methodically
> eats the host alive; more nature's norm than anomaly.
> ('Tarantula Hawk Wasp')

That nature has a sting is nothing new, but the weight on one side of these scales seems to be irredeemable where 'The corpse flower, a flower straight out of hell' shows man's continuous, systematic destruction of the natural habitat reduced in simple, equation-like language –

> Meanwhile, the forests of Sumatra and Borneo
> are being cleared. Ergo the corpse flower also.
> ('Rafflesia arnoldii')

There is little that is overtly political in *No More Time* and yet, when we read this work, we are left with a very strong sense that church and state are Gaia's inescapable enemies –

> When statecraft
> bands with religion, there's no better witchcraft.
> ('Zanzibar Leopard')

Berryman was not slow to engage in this sphere as we can see in his 1970 'Conversation' with the critic Richard Kostelanetz when he said –

> The current American society would drive anybody out of his skull, anybody who is at all responsive; it is almost unbearable... From public officials we expect to get lies, and we get them in profusion.
> (*Conversation with Berryman: Massachusetts Review 11 lines 340-347, 1970*)

Coming towards the end of the war in Vietnam and just over a half a century out from Donald Trump's disastrous climate policy (amongst others), Berryman's politics lay in the maelstrom of his public and private persona. Delanty is more subtle when, visiting the Vietnam War Memorial with a friend, he imagines –

> That mirroring wall: the litany
> of names on shiny black stone.
>
> I say nothing, imagine such a wall
> listing plants and creatures since Noah
> that we've undone, a roll call.
> ('On a Friend Visiting the Vietnam War Memorial')

The loss of all the 'plants and creatures since Noah' that is prompted by the Vietnam war dead detonates a myriad of metaphoric associations – a spiral of regret, loss, frustration and sadness that also reflects the *under voice* of this collection on the poetic, political and environmental levels.

The terza rima is a very difficult form to engage with in the English language. The superfluity of word endings in Italian, in particular, with the letters a, e, i and o to generate rhyme lends a breadth and versatility that English does not effectively possess. That Delanty can achieve such a unified focus on his world view using, judiciously, American and Corkonian slang, and wearing the overalls of terza rima, is a remarkable achievement and one that, to the best of my knowledge, no other Irish writer has done before.

No More Time is an important collection of poems. It is not only an alarm call based on passionately-held convictions, but a brave engagement with a notoriously difficult poetic form in terza rima. John Keats' twin components where poetry 'should... soothe the cares and lifts the thoughts of man' is only half achieved with the latter in this collection. There is nothing soothing or complacent in these poems. Ultimately, *No More Time* is a challenge to us all, perhaps best exemplified in 'Counting' from Part 2, *Breaking News*:

> thinking how fast
> the hummingbird beats its wings at the votive,
> 50 times a second and not just up-and-down,
> but each time rotating their wings in a figure 8,
> which means there's no start or end to each beat,
> storing sweetness in their ruby throats.
> Tell them they don't count. Tell them
> They're nothing.
> Now, tell yourself.

Finally, we can return to William Carlos Williams who said 'Poetry is creation of new form.' Dante's terza rima is, perhaps, the greatest example of form being forged to accommodate, in his case, a spiritual journey where the idiomatic prevailed. There are scant few other examples of this in literature, but Delanty's *No More Time*, in similar vein, complements the clarion call of our time – to protect and cherish what is left. This is no more telling than in Delanty's dedication of the collection to 'all those who work to slow climate change' and to say to following generations that 'some of the people gone before you are trying not to let you down.'

It seems that we too have 'passed the watchman on his beat', but Delanty is not 'unwilling to explain'. Anyone who is in touch (or wishing to be) with the probing pulse of contemporary poetry should read this collection.

W S Milne

Poetry Matters

Rory Waterman: *Sweet Nothings* (Carcanet Press, 2020)
Patrick Wright: *Full Sight Of Her* (Eyewear Publishing, 2020)
David Cooke: *Sicilian Elephants* (Two Rivers Press, 2021)
Josephine Balmer: *Ghost Passage* (Shearsman Books, 20220

The title of Rory Waterman's book is, of course, ironic. Although the poems are concerned with absence, loss, exile, the void, and so on, the implication is that we are not to take these themes too seriously (but, of course, we do). After all, the cliché, 'sweet nothings', implies words of affection exchanged by lovers as well as false promises (and the tone of the poems sometimes steps close to the neighbouring echo, following not far behind, of 'sweet FA'). The latter voice is heard throughout Waterman's satirical take on 'wokeness' in academia (especially in Literature departments) in his eponymous portraits of the lecturer Dr Bob Pintle (the Jacobean word for 'penis') and his Dean of Faculty at the University of Peterborough, Dr Jim Jones (namesake of the infamous American preacher who led his cult followers to their own immolation in the Jonestown Massacre – the implication is clear, of course, that he is leading the department down the primrose path to hell.) One has the feeling that Dr Jones does not know the meaning of the word 'pintle', and that he has never heard of Jim Jones.

After his failure to take on board his new Vice Chancellor's agenda of '"Globalisation"/(foreign students)', 'Employability'//and, just for him, a new '"Professionalism of Writing" module, whatever the fuck that is', Dr Pintle's application for a sabbatical is rejected on the grounds that it is not sufficient to take time off 'just to write poems'. He is advised by Dr Jones to attend a 'Winning Support for Sabbatical Workshop', and to ensure that his '4* REF Output Agreement/and book contract are both attached to the email,/with endorsement from two Student Reps and your Mentor'. Dejected, Dr Pintle daydreams a reply:

> *Hi Jim*, Bob pecks, then deletes. *Dear Jim, Oh YES!*
> *I'll write with that! Those sabbaticals: who got them?*
> *And have those colleagues had thirteen previous years*
> *on what you term 'the front line'? Anyway, Cheers!*
> *When I find time, I'll thank you in a poem,*

and place it in the fucking TLS...
He sighs. Holds backspace till all his work is gone.
The cursor blinks along with his catharsis,
And he stabs *Dear Jim, That's excellent! Thanks, Bob.*

His only relief is that he doesn't teach Chaucer or Shakespeare (they've been cancelled from the curriculum, along with the lecturers in Medieval and Elizabethan Studies), and is told he must scrap *The Waste Land* ('whitest malest privilege' according to the 'Equality and Inclusion' process) and *Briggflatts* ('a work of heteronormativity') but stick with Carol Ann Duffy's *The Bees* ('the gender balance' there is just right). The only question he is asked by a student in a seminar is, 'How do I get a First?' At that point all the other students (the three who have turned up out of a possible eleven) wake up. It's all very funny (if bleak) and reminded me of Kingsley Amis's *Lucky Jim*.

There is a much gentler tone to the other poems in the volume, concerned, for instance, with his early student days, summer jobs, counselling for depression, and so on. One perhaps can hear the kind of poem Dr Pintle would like to write, if he had the time, in Waterman's wonderful 'Harrier?':

Deergrass and alder and rowan, and roe deer
strutting behind them, and wrens everywhere
yapping and hidden, and grass of Parnassus
spread, dull meadowsweet for the year...

But he'd still have to explain what he was going on about. And where, in God's name, is Parnassus? The one exception to the gentleness is the poem entitled 'Like Father' which bravely confronts the trauma of growing up with a famous father who was violent and abusive. Waterman has written about this poem on *The Friday Poem* website, discussing how hard it was to write on such a private theme, and the difficulty of making that confession public: 'The things he said rarely matched up very well with the things I was beginning to see or think for myself', the growing boy beginning to realise just who his father was, and what he was like. But it is the honesty and courage which stays in the reader's mind on reading this poem, recounting memories of that violence – an anxious child

Who later found the custody hearing documents
while helping his mother clear her musty attic:
the affidavits of all his ex-dad's lovers,
each emphatic

that *I'm sure the child's interests are best served*
by being kept from this abusive man,
a drunk who bullied and hit me; his arrest statement
       from when my Nan

lost her front teeth (I hadn't been told the reason).

The irony is that his father too was a poet, and the poem ends: 'And I was trying to be like him – a bit,/in fewer and fewer ways – and started a poem/and this is it.' The poem acts as a kind of confessional catharsis, but is nevertheless very harrowing to read. Katy Evans-Bush has rightly said that the poem deserves 'a standing ovation'.

*

The title of Patrick Wright's *Full Sight Of Her* comes from John Milton's sonnet, 'Methought I saw my late espoused saint', an elegy for his wife: 'Yet once more I trust to have/Full sight of her in Heaven'. John McAuliffe has written movingly about the book, that it takes the reader 'to fearful, anxious places, describing love and care which come under terrible pressure. Wright's bereaved, often bereft poems, find words to protect the self, this lover who must become a "widower, prizing thumbnails"'. Siobhan Campbell has written that the book 'conveys a powerful sense of shared humanity', and Patricia McCarthy that it 'cuts to the very heart of loss'. It is difficult to single out any of these excellent, tender poems, but one that stays in my memory is a portrait, or vignette, of the poet combing his ailing wife's hair:

All that's left now
is the style, and I start back with the comb,
fan out a fringe as she watches TV.
The filaments are the days we've got left.
Roots of silver I cover with cosmic blue…

This gentle, moving tone is sustained throughout the volume (with some moments of bitterness and anger), with loving detail cherished or recalled. He has unbounded admiration for his wife's abilities as an artist: 'I love your tumbleweed moments…/how you turn an Ikea nightmare into/something Japanese', her skill in turning the ordinary into the miraculous. He praises her endurance and bravery in confronting imminent blindness:

How is it you see through your pinhole?
…You tell me the blind world is beautiful,
that once it's possible to get past the fear,
everything becomes cossetted, inward…

These moments she calls '*numens*', 'invoking all that's lost in the world'. It is in recalling such moments that, after her death, the poet's grief hits hardest:

Without you, I lose myself in the damask of sheets,
down a valium, slip into dream,
where cheek-to-cheek selfies stay intact.
Bank Holiday sirens, fading out.

I want days never to begin…

In another poem he writes:

Now the treatments have passed

I see the shape of Wales in the clouds. You tell me 'to go there,
anywhere but here.' *Just days now*. Where we, a pair condemned,

gaze different ways. Now the treatments have passed, your fingers
fidgeting craft won't say how you feel. Your thoughts, a country

I cannot reach…

In 'The Bitter End' he writes bravely, cursing the cancer:

No, this will never beat us,
when she's moaning, rocking for morphine.
I say to *you* — who's insidious,
hides cowardly along the linings of organs—
that love will win, love will grow stronger
with each howl it puts her through.
Love will win, it *must*…

These poems are a testament that love does win through, that art does matter, as his wife keenly knew – that these elegies matter. The tone, in its defiance, is close to John Donne's 'Death, be not proud', and the comparison stands in terms of the quality of the poems. Of recent books this one stands out for me, and can be ranked alongside Douglas Dunn's *Elegies*. It is a tremendous achievement, and must be congratulated. It must have been a difficult book to write.

*

Catriona O'Reilly has written of David Cooke's 'European sensibility', and Neil Fulwood of his 'innate poetic ability to study the everyday', qualities very much to the fore in his most recent book, *Sicilian Elephants*, where he explores the skin of the earth (*'la piel e la tierra'*, quoting Pablo Neruda in the epigraph to the book) that is Europe, and focusing precisely and movingly on the quotidian realities we often miss in our hurried inattentiveness. The book opens with a fine poem on ants which reminded me of Heine's poem on the death-watch beetle scuttling behind skirting-boards, then immediately moves on from the domestic to the public scene in the next poem, to the end of empire, to 'the tattered flags and atlas/where page by dusty page/the red has bled away'. There follows a wonderful poem about trees, incorporating David Hockney, Yeats and the Biblical Flood, but mainly I read it as a homage to Gerard Manley Hopkins's superb poem, 'Binsley Poplars', Cooke expecting his reader to be aware of such a tradition whilst writing brilliantly in his own voice. This is a quality which runs throughout the whole book. The idea of the skeletons of dwarf elephants found on the island of Sicily suggests that bulk is not everything, that the finest aspects of life are often captured in miniature, framed or hedged in the space of fine lyrics such as Cooke's poems, for instance. The elephants may have suffered from a lack of resources (hence their small size) but still they survived, endured, perhaps against the dictates of evolution. So it is culture, civilisation (here mainly that of Mediterranean Europe) survives against all the brutal odds. There are poems set in Venice, Sirmione, Gibraltar, Sicily, Barcelona, Casablanca, Vigo, and so on, catching the brilliant Mediterranean light and the mores of those cultures. Set side by side with these are poems on everyday, domestic subjects such as DIY, gardening ('Snipping, pruning, hacking', getting the roses right as he does his poems), shopping, cooking, children growing up and moving away from home, stamp-collecting and bird-watching with his son, thinking back on his childhood hobbies, and so on. I found these personal poems as moving and as substantial as the more public ones. The poet's aesthetic is a hopeful one, a desire for peace and resolution in a divisive and brutal world, a Platonic life spent 'deciphering/the shadows on the walls/of dungeons, caves,/and bleak ancestral halls'. The hope, however, is qualified by the intrusion of realities :'Our visionary towers/have crumbled... till all we had was slogans, flags, rubble;/our streets scoped by snipers' as he puts it in 'Ruins', a re-working of the Anglo-Saxon poem, 'The Ruin', where 'the work of giants has decayed'. There is a fine paean to Houdini, and others who practise legerdemain (including poets), spicing the humdrumness of life. What I like most about David Cooke's poetry is his attention to detail, and his capacity to freshen our outlook on the visible world. In this he is like a great short story writer who searches out the things that most of us miss, who reminds us that it is often in the shadows that things live most. He writes:

> I'm digging up the lavender hedge I coaxed
> from almost nothing all those years ago —
> ...checking for signs
> of growth, fussing, tamping, watching...
>
> Preoccupied elsewhere, in time
> the cosseting had to stop. Season by season,
> the hedge was left to fend for itself —
> woody, gnarled and, in the end, intractable.
>
> (from 'Lavender')

The world goes on without us, recalcitrant, unpredictable, but that is where its beauty lies, in its *otherness*, and the serious poet, as Nietzsche has said (in *The Genealogy of Morals*) finds a form that confronts, challenges and shapes that fact. David Cooke is just such a poet:

> In the road a dominant stag ponders.
>
> One day his kind will repossess it all.
> For now his antlers are like a chalice
> abrim with dingy light. High above him
> there's darkness, where tonight he dreams of stars.
>
> (from 'Urban')

Sicilian Elephants demonstrates that poetry matters, not just as performance, but as words on the page – the best words in the best order, as Coleridge said.

*

Like her earlier book of poetry, *The Paths of Survival* (2017), in *Ghost Passage* Josephine Balmer is interested in what she calls 'the urgent chain of humanity', the links and continuities which connect us over the centuries, concentrating in this case on the archaeological finds of Roman London – engravings from tombstones, tiles, clay lamps, a child's leather sole, what lies beneath the dark earth, all the shards preserved in wood, clay and stone, material elements which tell us much about our history. This historical perspective is represented, brought to life at different angles, with a particularity, a rich economy of style which shapes a new reality of living voices from the Roman era of occupation. The poems, based on fragments, express a world, a way of life, recording the physical and cultural world of a society at a particular time in history, an interlacing of words, lives and destructiveness 'to give a feeling of the reality of the speaker... a constantly felt dramatic voice' (Ezra Pound's words on his own technique in *The Cantos*). So it is Balmer presents vestiges, traces of Roman life in London, 'the hoard of forgotten worlds' as she phrased it in *The Paths of Survival,* the vulnerability, the fragility of the citizens' and slaves' lives, bringing a culture back to life through their idiosyncratic voices:

The cries of butchers in the market halls,
haze of blacksmiths, hum of metalworkers;
a scent of spice from across the empire,
stench of piss trickling out from tanners' stalls.

The swell of every language: Gallic, Greek,
German, Numidian, Thracian, Phrygian.
The swagger of swollen businessmen
claiming their ownership of our coined streets.

We hear the voices of brewers and tavern owners, of accountants and policemen, of builders and tourists, of teachers and lawyers. We hear of Britons learning 'new letters, new tools', of homesick Romans, Greeks and Gauls, of educators teaching the native 'savages' 'to sooth the jagged edge' of their dialect. One shard reveals a callous note regarding the sale of a slave-girl ('*Make hard coin out of soft flesh*'), a foreshadowing perhaps of the later British Empire when the colonised became the colonisers, highlighting that sense of historical continuity which is always at the forefront of Balmer's aesthetic. This is not an egregious comment, as one Cicero (Minor) notes 'I'd found subdued villages, smoke / scrolled up like fading stylus strokes', and one Roman describes the Thames as 'this filthy, sluggish/northern river'. This evocation of the spirit of the past reminded me of Marlow's words in Joseph Conrad's *Heart of Darkness,* that 'we live in the flicker of history', and how the Romans ('a wonderful lot of handymen') encountered 'savages' when they first came to Britain, 'the uttermost ends of the earth', to extend their empire.

We see ex-pats seeking new business, new fortunes being made (having been 'priced out of Rome'), merchants selling 'Syrian glass' and 'tessarae for mosaics' (which reminded me a little of David Jones's *The Tribune's Visitation* and *The Sleeping Lord*). One very moving fragment is that of a child's leather sole with the word '*Hector*' stamped on it. This is how a loved one is acknowledged and remembered, and the brief name serves as a telling epitaph. The homely artefacts which are unearthed serve as symbols in the sequence, much as they do in Rilke's *Duino Elegies*, where jugs, gates, fruit-trees, windows serve to emphasise our passing signatures. The messages engraved on marble slabs, writing tablets, clay pots, tiles, flagons, jewellery and amulets give us an imagined insight into various lives and occupations. There is much more to the sequence than I can outline here, but an additional thrill to reading the book lies with the useful historical notes and sources listed by the poet, facts gleaned from excavations, reports, epitaphs, and so on, giving us information on 'the first generation of Londoners'. I also like the way in which the wonderful cover to the book (a reproduction of 'a tiny carved cameo seal, dating from the third century CE and found on the Thames foreshore') leads us into the heart of the city of London itself.

In *Ghost Passage* Poetry and History (Euterpe and Clio) meet, not competing for once, but brilliantly fused and celebrated. It is a book worth returning to time and again.

Translations/Versions

'Wires' by Marina Tsvetaeva translated by Belinda Cooke.

Marina Tsvetaeva (1992-1941) is considered one of the greatest twentieth century Russian poets. She lived through and wrote of the Russian Revolution of 1917 and the Moscow famine that followed, where her younger daughter died of starvation. She then left Russia in 1922 and lived with her family in increasing poverty in Berlin, Prague and Paris before returning to Russia in 1939. Her husband Sergei Efron and remaining daughter Ariadna Efron were arrested on espionage charges in 1941. Her husband was executed and her daughter imprisoned for a number of years. Increasingly isolated, Tsvetaeva committed suicide in 1941, leaving only her son George who died shortly after, fighting in the Soviet army against the German invasion.

Tsvetaeva's 'Wires' from *After Russia* is a perfect example of her unique style. This collection explores her years of exile with endless, highly innovative motifs on the notion of movement and sound: pedals, oars, Scythian arrows, shells – all conveyed with often unconventional syntax, and creative wordplay. Gugliemo Marconi had sent the first wireless transmission across the Atlantic in 1901, and by the 'twenties this had transformed communication. Tsvetaeva draws on this innovation to defy the pain of exile with this hauntingly emotional sequence on separation from her poetic soulmate Boris Pasternak — best known in the west for his novel *Dr Zhivago* – poems that show her fragmentary style at its most effective.

Wires
(a selection)

> *Des Herzens Woge schäumte nicht*
> *so schön empor und würde Geist,*
> *wenn nicht der alte stumme Fels,*
> *das Schicksal, ihr entgegenstande.*
> *Holderin*[1]

i

Along rows of singing wires
propping up the heavens
I send you my share
of earthly dust.

---

[1] 'The heart's wave would not transform so beautifully to foaming spirit, if it was not forced to confront rock's fateful, silent intransigence.

                    Along this avenue
of breaths – this telegraphic
pole to pole I send out: I l-o-v-e y-o-u...

I implore you, (I don't *write* it –
wires are more intimate) up here
where Atlas has installed
a hippodrome
for sky dwellers...

                    this is my tele-
graphic g-o-o-d b-y-e....

Can you hear it? It is the last outburst
before coming hoarse: f-o-r-g-i-v-e m-e...
the rigging over seas of cornfields,
a soft Atlantic path:

higher, higher – merging into
Ariadne's: r-e-t-u-r-n...

Look back!...it is the cries of the depressed
from cheap hospitals: *I won't get out,*
the final farewells to the dying,
Hades voices ringing through

steel wires then fading away... the distance
putting a curse on us: *Feel some p-i-t-y....*

Take pity on me! (Can you make it out
in all this choir?) in the expiring shout
of stubborn passions —
just a breath of Eurydice:

up through the soil the sudden r-i-s-e...
Eurydice's *Forget my fate,*
but ah! Remember me...

ii

How can I tell you in metre and rhyme?
The heart's so much wider.
You'd need the whole of Racine or Shakespeare,
to even get close.

'Anyone will weep at a wound...
cry out at a snake among the roses'...
but for Phaedra there was only Hippolyte
and for Ariadne Theseus.

There's no limit to a heart torn to shreds –
you can be sure, that in losing you,
I have lost count of those I've lost
in space and time – the *absent* lovers.

How can we speak of hope,
when the air I breathe is filled with you?
Since I feel my bones are like Naxos.
Since I feel the blood in my veins is like the Styx.

There is a desert inside me. With my eyes closed
it is a bottomless place, outside of days, its dates
lying off the calendar...
                    Severed from you,
I am neither Ariadne nor...
                              what loss!

Blind and unseeing, along which
seas and towns should I look for you?
I believe only in wires connected to wires –
propped up on the telegraph wire I weep.

iii

Paths

Rifling through and rejecting all –
semaphore above all – that wildest
cacophony of schools ...of spring thaws,
where, whole choir in tow, I would –

163

fling my sleeves like banners...
shamelessly – and still now
I hum with the lyrical wires
of my high passions.

Telegraph pole. Is there not
a shorter route? Know that
while the sky remains –
                    (transmitter of feeling,
            herald of tangible lips...)

while the heavens remain,
dawns edging over the horizon,
everywhere, distinct and enduring,
I will bind myself to you.

Through the epoch's evil years,
its endless lies and mounting debris,
come my unpublished sighs
my frenzied passion...

Telegrams are no use – blunt
and fixed, with their urgent stamping,
for us rather, spring's deluge, its gutters
of mud, its endless wire spaces.

iv

Despotic suburb.
Telegraph wires.

O how I have longed for this,
my high-flown shout from the womb
to the wind – my heart, like
a magnetic spark of metre.

What of metre and measure?
The fourth dimension takes its revenge –
rushing over mortal metrics with
perjuries it gives a whistle –

Ssh – listen! Are there wires and poles
everywhere? The brow strains to hear,
know these difficult words
are nothing more than the cry

of the nightingale having lost its path...
(What use is the world without a loved one?)
...having fallen in love with the lyre of your hands,
the Leila of your lips.

Five poems from Paul Éluard's *Last Love Poems (Derniers Poèmes d'Amour)* translated by Timothy Adès

Paul Éluard 1895–1952 was known worldwide as the Poet of Freedom
when his poem 'Liberté' was dropped massively into France by the RAF. He was a founder of dadaism and surrealism, and twice joined the Communist Party. Often sickly and in hospital, he was a great campaigner for peace and liberty. He overcame all obstacles to marry 'Gala' (Diakonova), his inspiration, who later left him for Dalí. He married 'Nusch' and was devastated by her sudden death. That is the background to these *Last Love Poems*.

Ecstasy

I am facing this feminine landscape
Like a child in front of the fire
Smiling vaguely tears in its eyes
This landscape where everything stirs in me
Where mirrors cloud where mirrors clear
Reflecting two naked bodies season by season

I've so many reasons to lose myself
On this roadless ground, under this heaven of no horizon
Fine reasons I didn't know yesterday
And will never forget
Fine keys of glances keys their own daughters
Facing this landscape where nature is mine

In front of the fire the first fire
Fine reason mistress

Star identified
On earth under heaven out of my heart in my heart

Second bud first green leaf
That the sea puts its wings over
And the sun right at the end coming from us

I am facing this feminine landscape
Like a branch in the fire.

Alive and Dead She is Apart

(…)
My hands my feet were hers
And my desires and my poem were hers
(…)
You had no business with death
(…)
My little bird is listening I'm here I'm at your side
(…)
I'm not asleep I fell I stumbled in your absence
I've no fire no strength near you
(…)
I suffer from your silence for ever
O my love.

Certainty

If I speak it's to hear you better
If I hear you I'm sure to understand you

If you smile it's to invade me better
If you smile I see the whole world

If I clasp you it's to continue myself
If we live all will be for pleasure

If I leave you we'll remember each other
In leaving you we'll rediscover each other

Negation of Poetry

I've had from you all the worry all the torment
That can be taken out of everything out of nothing
Could I have failed to love you
You whom kindness of heart
Like a peach after another peach
As succulent as summer

All the worry all the torment
Of living on and being absent
Of writing this poem

Instead of the living poem

Which I won't write
Since you're not there

The slightest sketches of fire
Prepare the ultimate conflagration
The smallest crumbs of bread
Are enough for the dying

I've known living virtue
I've known incarnate good
I reject your death but I accept my own
Your shade spreading over me
I'd like to make it into a garden

The arc is split up we're of the one same night
And I want to continue your immobility
And the non-existent discussion
That begins with you and will end in me
With me wilful stubborn rebellious
Loving as you do the delights of this earth.

My dead one alive

In my grief nothing is in motion
I am waiting, no-one will come
Not by day, not by night
Nor ever beyond what was myself

My eyes have separated from your eyes
They lose their confidence, they lose their light
My lips have separated from your lips
My lips have separated from pleasure
And from the sense of love, and from the sense of life
My hands have separated from your hands
My hands allow everything to slip away
They will not move forward, there is no more road
They will not know my tally, will not know repose

I am granted to see my life at an end
Along with yours
My life in your power
And I thought it was infinite

And the future my only hope is my tomb
Just like yours, caught in an uncaring world
I was so close to you that I feel cold near to others.

Will Stone

A Note on Monique Saint-Hélier and Rilke

Monique Saint-Hélier (1895-1855) was the pen name of Monique Briod, an author from the Francophone region of western Switzerland. She was best known in the French literary world during the 1930s for her novel concerning ill-starred lovers, *Bois-Mort*, published in 1934 by Grasset, the success of which lead to her being proposed for the Goncourt and Fémina literary prizes. Monique was constantly harassed throughout her life by ill health and disability. Having moved in 1926 from Switzerland to Paris with her husband Blaise Briod, she was obliged to write from her bed or a chaise-longue, like Proust with whom elements of her writings have been compared. The war years proved a particular challenging period for the physically compromised author and her husband after Monique underwent a major operation in 1939 followed by the trauma of their failed attempt to flee occupied Paris in 1940. But during those dark days Monique applied herself to writing her intimate and revealing journal which has recently been published in its entirety (1895-1955) by Éditions de l'Aire. Despite further works appearing in the post-war period, including the important *Correspondance 1944-55* edited by Jean Paulhan, Monique Saint-Hélier's presence began to fade and though obstinately continuing to write, she succumbed to the effects of a heart attack in March 1955.

In 1923 after a prolonged period of invalidity in a Bern clinic, Monique Briod had encountered the poet Rainer Maria Rilke for the first time at a ball held in the city during early summer. Not able to read German it is unlikely that she was then familiar with his poetry. Until Rilke's death three years later, the Swiss woman of letters maintained a vital correspondence, underscored by a genuine friendship with the great poet. Her proximity to Rilke in those years almost certainly eased her subsequent passage into the Parisian literary world. In 1927 she published *À Rilke pour Noël* (Éditions du Chandelier) and in 1935 her 'Souvenir de Rilke' appeared in *La Revue Universelle,* Paris.

Rilke

To Monique St Hélier

Do you recall those things we lost yesterday?
One last time, they implore you
in vain
to remain close beside you.
But the angel of loss brushes them with distracted wing:
we can hold them no more, we stop them.
They have received, without us knowing when,
the mark of absence,
in spite of windows fastened, a wind, subtle
advances towards them.
They will take leave of this precise order
of the possession that names them;
soon what will be their life
that will no more be the life of man
who so long loved them? Will they too
harbour deep regrets amidst the mournful dusts?
Or is it that things
help us toward a more timely
forgetting? The obscure joy to be matter
draws them back, hands them to the blind mother
who touches them and scarcely reproaches them
for having suffered human thought.

Translated by Will Stone

Robert Selby

Rainer Maria Rilke: *Poems to Night*, translated and with an introduction by Will Stone (Pushkin Press, £12)

At the end of 1916, Rainer Maria Rilke – exiled by war from his beloved Paris to Germany – presented Rudolf Kassner with a notebook of 22 new poems entitled *Gedichte an die Nacht* (*Poems to Night*). In his translation of this sequence (Pushkin Press, 2020), Stone explains that Rilke hoped the poems would reassure Kassner, a longstanding friend, of 'the continuation of his creative endeavour' despite a collapse in confidence – likely partly attributable to Europe's descent into conflict – which had suspended his progress on what would become the more famous existential sequence, the *Duino Elegies*. Rilke wrote the first poems of *Poems to Night* while exploring Ronda, Spain in early 1913 and the last in Paris just five months before war commenced. Stone's important new edition brings all the poems in the sequence together in English for the first time and also includes seven related drafts or fragments, plus fifteen night-themed poems selected from Rilke's other works.

According to Stone, Rilke had originally considered having *Poems to Night* form a second section of the *Duino Elegies*, and there is indeed some commonality of themes and ideas between them, but he warns: 'They are more actively hermetic, as if enfolding themselves and thus demanding of the reader an even greater concentration'. Furthermore, they 'possess the aura of a clandestine text, and resist any assured interpretation'. It is hard to read *Poems to Night* and not feel that, if it was Rilke's attempt to prove his concentration had not been understandably scattered by world events, it fails to convince. Michael Hofmann has memorably written of Rilke that 'even by the standard of unworldly poets, he is like one of those cabinet ministers who doesn't know the price of milk'; Rilke's poetry can sometimes strain at the buoy of intelligibility and in *Poems to Night* it often becomes unmoored. Few of the poems are about actual *things* and we are left to make do with mood and atmosphere, or what Stone more patiently calls an 'arcane aura' of 'organic indecipherability'. The sense of a great poet off his A-game, or making notes for his A-game, is sharpened by the presence, at the rear of the edition, of superior night-themed poems from Rilke's other works, many written in happier times – though not exclusively. 'At Night I wish to converse with the angel' ('Can you see Eden? / Then I must say: Eden is on fire'), written in Irschenhausen in the second month of war, demonstrates that his gift had not been lost for good.

For Rilke, Stone explains, night represented 'a celestial gateway or enacting space between inner and outer reality', with angels the mediators in this dialogue with transcendence:

So, now it will be the angel
who drinks slowly from my features
the wine-enlightened face.
Thirsting, who signalled you to come?

There is much talk of faces, features, smiles and brows, and angels drinking from them. The night sky itself is a 'high mountain range' of stars, to feel insignificant under, to lose oneself in ('the compressed feelings scatter like stars, / as if a posy of blooms were untied') or feel consoled by ('Rather than into pillows, / weep upwards') – after all, the indifferent heavens are 'powerful, thronged with lions, / who to us remain inscrutable'. Lovely lines, and this, ultimately, is what *Poems to Night* is: beams of memorable lucidity intermittently penetrating a wider murk. Pushkin have made a beautiful edition of it and Stone's introduction is characteristically incisive and sensitive, while the poems themselves set the pulses racing.

Martyn Crucefix

Durs Grünbein: *Porcelain*, tr. Karen Leeder (Seagull Books, 2020)

Ulrike Almut Sandig: *I Am a Field Full of Rapeseed, Give Cover to Deer and Shine Like Thirteen Oil Paintings Laid One on Top of the Other*, tr. Karen Leeder (Seagull Books, 2020)

For a writer who has published over thirty books of poetry and prose in his native Germany, we have had too little of Durs Grünbein in English. Michael Hofmann's *Ashes for Breakfast* (2005) introduced some of the earlier work and described Grünbein as possessed of melancholia, amplitude, a love of Brodsky, a love of the Classics, plus wide-ranging interests in medicine, neuroscience, contemporary art and metaphysics. John Ashbery praised Grünbein, identifying his subject as 'this life, so useless, so rich' and the challenge to any translator is precisely this breadth and ambition. Happily, Karen Leeder is proving to be a really fine conduit for Grünbein's work and here she triumphantly tackles his 2005 sequence of poems about the firebombing of his hometown, Dresden, by American and British planes in February 1945. This book has very deservedly just won the Sclekeltieck prize, 2022.

Porcelain is a sequence of forty nine poems, ten lines each, rhymed and grounded in Classical metre and given an air of Classical elegy by its subtitle, 'Poem on the Downfall of My City' ('Poem vom Untergang meiner Stadt'). But if resolution, consolation or summing-up might be expected, this is, definitively, not what we get. The title, of course, refers to the Meissen pottery which, from the eighteenth century on, brought Dresden its great wealth and fame. But it is also a pun on the poet to whom the sequence is dedicated: Paul Celan. In Celan's poem 'Your eyes embraced' there is an effort to swallow the ashes of genocide but they return to the throat as 'Ash- / hiccups', an image repeated in Grünbein's opening poem: "It comes back like hiccups: elegy". The sequence does indeed hiccup in the sense of its jerky shifts of tone, its multifaceted images of Grünbein himself and in its close to choking articulation of the horrors of the Dresden bombing.

A self-conscious awkwardness or self-questioning is clear from the start: 'Why complain, Johnny-come-lately? Dresden was long gone / when your little light first appeared'. Grünbein was born seventeen years after the bombing and accepts he cannot 'witness' the event in any simple way. But personal details do surface in the sequence such as in poem 8 where the young boy grows familiar with the still evident urban destruction: 'proud and mute . . . the ravaged city'. He senses something of 'that glory passed away' but can hardly know 'the things [his] mother saw, / scarcely five years old' (poem 10). Later poems remember moments when his mother's doll was in danger of the flames ('Flames as high as houses sucked the air along the streets'), but was rescued, unscathed, 'or that is what they say' (poems 40/41). Leeder explains in her Introduction that Grünbein has been criticised in part for a sentimentality and this is perhaps such a moment. But the indication that this is reportage (family reportage at that) gives permission for sentiment and Grünbein is fully conscious of (and in control of) the massive swings in tone through the whole sequence. Poem 48 is one that might also lay itself open to charges of sentiment, focusing on a pair of lovers (Martha and Heinrich) seemingly caught up in the devastation: 'Kids, the pair of you, first kisses in the thick of war, / until you met that night you'd grown up in uniform'. But Grünbein works repeatedly through allusiveness and intertextuality, so this Romeo and Juliet trope is hardened and complicated when we hear that, not only was the German air defence's grid reference for Dresden code-named 'Martha-Heinrich 8', but also that both names recall characters in Goethe's *Faust*.

In poem 38, Grünbein seems equally aware that some of his images of Dresden after the bombing might be open to the same criticism of a hyper-emotional tone. 'Five long weeks upon the Altmarkt square, the horses / scratched the straw and watched the griddled corpses / burn. Mawkish? Ach, give over, late-born soul'. As this example shows, the sequence does confront the horrors unleashed on the city as in poem 22: 'Are those people popping like chestnuts between / the gutted trams?' But looked at more carefully, even this grisly observation is nominally from the perspective of a stone angel on the cathedral roof. It is this continual innovation and manipulation of perspective that is important to the poems' purpose and how we should read them.

One important perspective Grünbein explores is the victim-narrative that predominated in thinking about the event in post-war East Germany and more recently. One aspect of this is the placing of the Dresden bombing in the historical context of German bombing of Warsaw in 1944 and the German's systematic persecution of the Jews. Dresden's fate did not rise *ex nihilo*. This latter myth, Grünbein embodies in the eroticisation of the bombing – the city as defenceless virgin – as in poem 45's image of the city and the Elbe: 'River like a sash of silver draped round her hips / enticing in the moonlight'.

From such examples, it's easy to see why Grünbein's own position on the bombing has been vociferously discussed and questioned. But he warns against using the destruction of the city as any kind of exemplum: 'Let Dresden be. You won't find what you are looking for' (poem 6). The reader understands he is also advising himself here, while, at the same time, acknowledging the human drive to interpret, to search for meaning, even in the most appalling events. The sequence's treatment of Arthur 'Bomber' Harris, the RAF Commander-in-Chief during the bombing of Dresden, is interestingly equivocal. Poem 4 alludes almost invisibly to Harris' comment on the Dresden bombing, when he suggested that objections to it were based on a sentimental image of the city as full of 'German bands and Dresden shepherdesses' when, in reality, it was a Nazi munitions and transportation centre. In fact, Harris was carrying out orders from Winston Churchill: 'No sweat, Arthur, you only did what you had to do' (poem 13). And in poem 23, Grünbein also notes that some more recent left-wingers in Germany have chanted 'Thank you, Harris!' in their efforts to question and counter more simplistic, victim-narrative commemorations of the event.

In such ways, *Porcelain* revels in its own pluralities while acknowledging and itself attempting to make some sense of an epitome of senseless destruction. The final line of the book plainly states the human need to avoid finality, the fall into fixity, yet accepts the compulsion to explain, to create meaning: 'Changing places, times, dimensions as he goes – goes on – creating". And behind all this stand those exquisite china objects, the 'white gold' that made the city rich and famous:

> Falconers are there, vintners, nymphs with conch-shell horns,
> frog-faced putti, figures riding seahorses and swans.
> Groups of shepherdesses, lovely gardeners, beasts of lore . . .
> Porcelain—most fragile thing

The collision of Allied bombs and Dresden's fragile porcelain lies at the heart of Grünbein's poem. There was no contest, of course, though some pieces and many fragments remained and were perhaps repaired. Grünbein's poems enact this process, collecting perspectives, often incongruous, even contradictory, but bringing them into relation with each other, not to make any definitive statement, but to hold up a mirror to us, to the recurrent tension between our need to create and our drive to destroy.

The eponymous figure from 'Hans im Glück', one of the stories in *The Children's and Household Tales of the Brothers Grimm* (1812), features in Grünbein's 11th poem. In the original, Hans has anything of value taken from him, bit by bit, yet he remains optimistic, refusing to acknowledge reality. Grünbein treats this is as a further image of the myth of Dresden as undeserving victim. Interestingly, the same figure appears in Ulrike Almut Sandig's collection, *I Am a Field Full of Rapeseed, Give Cover to Deer and Shine Like Thirteen Oil Paintings Laid One on Top of the Other* (also translated by Karen Leeder). But Sandig's presentation of Hans is more poignant, less ironic, as even the boy's language is stripped from him and he tries to write a letter to a loved one: 'what are you up to? // + esp: where r u? / ru ru // ru'. In the context of the full collection, the boy might be thought of as a refugee, forcibly having his culture and language stripped from him, though one of the strengths of the poem is that it also works as an updated fairy tale, a little myth of loss and diminished presence with more universal application. Such re-purposing of several of Grimm's tales is one of the most striking things about this collection. Sandig announces in another poem, 'we find ourselves deep in the future of fairy tale' ('the sweet porridge') and she, like Angela Carter before her, redeploys the fairy tale's surreal narratives, bold characterisation, its humour and violence, its symbolism and moral intensity for her own purposes.

The other striking aspect of Sandig's writing here is her bold linguistic and formal choices. There is an absence of punctuation, capitalisation, of poem titles (bolded phrases mid-poem often serve as titles), of conventional forms, of a clear lyric 'I', of plainly pursued narratives. This results in radically shifting ground for the reader which can be both bewildering and exciting. Several poems indicate these choices are firmly rooted in issues of epistemology and ideas concerning personal identity. So, the opening poem, 'from the wings', ambitiously sets out a complete life from 'screaming' beginning to its 'silent' conclusion. The interim is portrayed as all fluidity, 'a stream that flows into others / while others again flow into it'. As much as there is any discrete self to be identified, 'I am made wholly of language', and the individual is a creature 'that must speak / to understand itself'. The self is also one of many 'fragile / greedy alpha-creatures' and understands itself to be, ultimately, 'a fluid tuning fork I am my own / song'. In the same vein, the book closes with 'where I am now', which sets the self metaphorically in some remote Arctic research station, a self that is at the same time a woman swimming in a municipal pool, moving freestyle through the water, 'parting the water before me', in an image of self-creation and open-ended exploration that, to some, will recall Eliot's 'Little Gidding': "We shall not cease from exploration".

This is, as it were, the metaphysical background to Sandig's vision and it gives rise to poems like 'I am the shadow for you to hide beneath' in which the narrative voice celebrates just such fluidity of identity in an address to "friends"/readers that has the quality of Whitman's 'I contain multitudes' (*Song of Myself*), though with a good deal more anxiety: 'every morning I get up and don't have a clue: / is it me, Almut? Ulrike?' This is also the poem containing the book's full title, 'I am a field full of rapeseed, give cover to deer / and shine like thirteen oil paintings laid one on top / of the other' and the poem goes on, in the name of radical fluidity, the 'I' as landscape, huntress, a text that begins to unravel just as it reaches an end, a soldier, a girl, a woman. Elsewhere, 'to be wood in a table', as the title suggests, continues the theme: 'not to be old and not to be young, but old / enough to be several things at once'. This includes the Rilkean desire for 'simple things like "tree"' as well as the freedom of having no name, 'no longer to say: "I am"'.

Such poems are both celebratory in tone, but also alertly defensive. The reason is that there are forces abroad, ways of seeing and their associated politics that offer counter narratives. So, the expected calm of 'lullaby for all those' is really a call to arms, or at least a call to resist. It is 'for all / those who put up a fight, when somebody / says: lights out, no more talking'. In a superb passage, once more Leeder's translation of the German is brilliant, the forces of 'DARKNESS' begin to emerge by implication:

> we're waiting for two
> or three of those good, humming dreams
> four peace treaties, five apples in deep sleep
> we are waiting for six cathedrals and for
> those seven fat cows, eight quiet hours
> full of sleep, we're waiting for nine friends
> gone missing. we're counting our fingers.
>
> we're still resisting. we won't go to sleep.

What is being resisted are the forces of repression, of fixity not fluidity, narrowness not breadth, fundamentalist conviction not open-endedness.

Sandig places a poem in the centre of the book which draws heavily on statements made by Pegida, Germany's populist, right wing, anti-immigration party. The text is full of rallying calls expressing a faith in clarity, mastery, resolution and purification: 'from now on / nothing will stand in our way, no language / we cannot master, we will strike out mistakes / and shake each other's freshly washed hands'. One of the Grimm's sourced poems, a sister speaking to her brother, presents a narrative of the boy's development into a threatening 'hunter'. Such a poem looks both ways towards the violence of neo-Nazis, but also towards the violent radicalisation of young jihadists.

Sandig's poems dealing more obviously with issues of state power, war, migration and displacement (especially hot topics in Germany, a country in the Schengen area of Europe and seen by some as an ideal destination – see the poem 'tale of the land of milk and honey') are particularly impressive.

The 'ballad of the abolition of night' draws on details of systematic torture prosecuted by the USA, 'a state lagging somewhat behind / on the historical timeline of our kind'. 'instructions for flying' revises statements leaflets distributed at the Idomeni refugee camp in 2016. The same camp, close to the borders of Greece, is the focus of another poem which expresses the poet's 'moral dismay'. The disquiet is partly at her own nation's equivocations about the refugee crisis (what if there's not a single / jot of good *Deutsch* to be found in this / *Land* of mine") but also personally, at finding rhymes but ultimately doing 'sweet FA'.

With Grünbein, Sandig is expressing the moral complexity in the face of man's inhumanity to man as much as any simplistic moral dismay. This is, in part, the subject of some of the Grimm poems (interestingly, in German, the word 'grimm' means 'anger, ire'). 'Grimm' itself opens optimistically, messages being scribbled onto raw eggs, but increasing urgency leads to extra pressure and the eggs break. Still, like Hans in luck, the narrator seems 'unfazed in / the crumbling ruins' though the final image is only of eggs smashed, 'a well-nigh limitless / supply of fragments and rage most grim'. But Sandig is an optimist, I think. Though couched in conditionals, 'news from the German language, 2026AD' works hard to portray a future of more settled diversity (Iraqi dates, Turkish honey, Syrian poetry). The opposing prospect is relegated to a parenthesis – if quite a long one. But hope has the final word: 'if it works, we, that's all of you and me, / will sing a lullaby, rhyme in unison [. . .] but more than that, we will be'.

David Cooke

Peter Huchel: *These Numbered Days* translated by Martyn Crucefix (Shearsman Books)

Peter Huchel (1903-1981) was born in Lichterfelde, a suburb of Berlin in the former German Democratic Republic. He lived through two world wars and, as a liberal humanist, was out of sympathy with the tenets of National Socialism. Unfortunately, even after the war, his situation scarcely improved. Viewed with suspicion by the communist regime, he was kept under surveillance for years and subjected to constant harassment. His poems first came to the attention of the English-speaking world in versions by Michael Hamburger in 1974. Then, in 1983, Anvil brought out *The Garden of Theophrastus*, Hamburger's updated and enlarged selection from the four collections which were published in his lifetime. Rather than simply putting together yet another selection from the entire range of Huchell's poetry, Martyn Crucefix has decided to translate in its entirety *Gezählte Tage/These Numbered Days*, Huchel's third collections written when he was at the height of his powers. This means that we have before us a book of poems arranged by the poet himself as a coherent whole, and we gain thereby a further insight to the poet's creative processes. Moreover, to adapt the words that Seamus Heaney once used when reviewing Osip Mandelstam's *Kamen/Stone*, it 'amplifies our sense of what *These Numbered Days* really meant to its contemporary readers.'

The opening poem, 'Ophelia', sets the tone: 'the probing of sticks,/ a curt command,/ they lift out a muddied / snare of barbed wire.' This is followed by 'Answer', the opening stanza of which is a good example of Huchel's brooding, laconic style and Crucefix's sure touch as a translator:

> Between two nights
> comes brief day.
> The farmyard remains.
> And for us, a trap set
> in the brake by the hunter.

Here is the same stanza in Hamburger's version:

> Between two nights
> the brief day.
> What remains is the homestead.
> And a trap the huntsmen
> set for us in the thicket.

Though both translators stick close to the original, it seems, to my ear at least, that Crucefix's version is rhythmically tighter and more musical, particularly in its concluding couplet.

Like his great predecessor Georg Trakl, Huchel creates allegorical landscapes. They are frequently bleak and comfortless. In 'Under the Constellation of Hercules', the poem opens with an image that conveys the isolation and seeming insignificance of humanity in this desolate expanse: 'A settlement, / no larger / than the circle / a buzzard traces / in the evening sky'. For much of his life, Huchel was an internal exile who spent years as more or less a prisoner in his own house. Consequently, his imagined world frequently mirrors the circumstances of his own everyday reality. Here he is in 'Exile':

Come evening, friends close in,
the shadows of hills.
Slowly they press across the threshold,
darkening the salt,
darkening the bread
and with my silence they strike up a conversation..

This is a place where one hunkers down and gets by as best one can. Outside there's a world haunted by shadows, where human existence is transitory and insecure. Even when Huchel casts his gaze towards the south he finds little comfort. In 'Venice in the Rain', he seems less struck by the city's grandeur than 'the long patience / of piles.'

Frequently setting the minutiae of human existence against the backdrop of history's ravaged landscapes, Huchel's poems have a strong affinity with those of the French poet Jean Follain who, also born in 1903, was his exact contemporary. There is no reason to presume that either knew the other's work but a poem like 'Cockscombs' could almost have been written by Follain:

One evening, after market,
an old woman offered
two young roosters.
All trussed up,
their feet tied,
heads to the ground,
they hung
limp
in her earthy hand.
I walked on.

Beyond the piers
of the bay
I catch in the reflection of the sinking sun,
cockscombs of jagged rocks
lit up in the water.

There is no getting away from it, Huchel is an austere poet, but what redeems his work is clarity of his images, its tight-lipped refusal to be beaten down. It is unsurprising then that he identifies with the vagabond poet François Villon, who was shunned as an outlaw, or with Alcaeus and Pe-Lo-Thien, both of whom rebelled against tyranny and were cast out into exile. In 'The Dipper', he draws a comparison between himself as a poet, trying to 'fish out a word' and the insignificant little bird who 'picks its food / from the stony bed of the river'.

Clear-sighted and dispassionate, Huchel's stoicism is doubtless informed by his experience as a conscript in the Second World War and the time he spent in Russia as a prisoner of war. This is most memorably expressed in 'Defeat', a substantial poem which is given a prominent place in the central section of this book:

Slowly the emptiness of night descended,
filled with the howling of dogs.
Defeat sank
into the frozen veins of the country.

By the time we have reached the final section of *These Numbered Days*, there are poems which are more obviously autobiographical. 'April '63' evokes a period when certain writers and filmmakers were denounced by the GDR government for their anti-communist views in an almost surreal rebranding of McCarthyism and the House Un-American Activities Committee which engaged in similarly pernicious denuciations a decade earlier in the United States, while in 'Hubertusweg' we are given an insight into life under the ceaseless gaze of the Stasi: 'What's in it for him, noting investigations / in his blue octavo book, my friends' car numbers ...' Huchel was a poet who, like Brecht, felt that he was living in 'dark times'. However, as Karen Leeder suggests in her elegant introduction to this collection, it may be that our days too are numbered, as we face an ecological crisis and a darkness that Huchel could hardly have imagined. Peter Huchel is a stunning poet, a poet who matters, and one who may have found in Martyn Crucefix his definitive translator.

CHOSEN BROADSHEET POET

Betty Doyle is a 27 year old poet from Merseyside. Her work has appeared in *Poetry Wales, Butcher's Dog, And Other Poems,* and *BRAG Magazine,* amongst others. She is currently studying for a PhD in Creative Writing at Manchester Metropolitan University, with her research focusing on infertility poetry. Her debut poetry pamphlet, *Girl Parts,* will be published by Verve Poetry Press in March 2022. Twitter: betty_poet

A Room in the First House

inspired by Anna Marie Tendler's series of
photographs, 'Rooms in the First House'

Darling, it's just how you like it.
The plump rugs spun by a grandmother,
dried lavender,
the wet red plush that rolls out for your arrival.
I have hung the Norman Rockwells,
soft lighting, chosen Mozart;
let the doctors bend and scrape away,
sear and purify my insides with their silver.
Somehow, in this flinty lottery of womanhood,
I have dodged all men
that threaten us. Somehow, I have sailed through
on the scallop shell of our ancestors,
through the bad crop and the boat over
and the nine dead babies and the bombs through the roof
to arrive: finding that
it is not how I left it,
back in my youth, when I was sure of the glass,
the tile, the timber; its four walls, all its curtains and lamps.
Now, all the windows are caved through,
and the one light left inside swinging
is blue. There's mould inside the rolling pin,
and cupboard doors lead to nowhere.
Fires do not light, and the carpet cannot reach the corners.
I sit at the head of an empty table, watching in real time
the milk curdle, the fruit wither, the candles snuff out.
This is all mine, not yours. This is all that I have.

Shaving My Face

A rite of passage, this is –
the ritualistic quiet conversation,
Father's head bowed above Son's,
rugged Madonna with Child.
All summer, the Son has been unfurling
outwards, from the tender pulp of
androgenous childhood, all limbs stretching
out from that simple mulch toward
the creation of man, little fingers elongating
like crocus sprouts beginning to peek
from February soil.
A voice, deepened. Shoulders, laden.
Ribs, outstretched, and a shadow
crossing a top lip, not following whatever
the sun did. Conscious of itself,
the way a crown or halo is, aware of its weight,
how it had been carried by grandfathers
over oceans and trenches,
and harbored by grandmothers,
through famines and bombs;
protected by countless, faceless people
to arrive here. The ceremony that survived.
The Father's hand on the Son's shoulder.
The door opening into chilly light.
The churn of lather, the shock of its cold
against the golden apples of small cheeks.
Ageless steel, the razor's bent head
that reveres *manhood, manhood* – its forever prayer.
There is no rite for the women, no celebration
into adulthood's umbral fault.
Only the whispers, the stares and points –
on the outside, in another shadow,
beyond tradition, the only Daughter.

Fruits of Labour

the huge bloom,
cherry shaped pain

the apples and pears
of my body,
my hips

the fruit of knowledge
throbbing red
in my gut, my chest, my head

in my loose billowing skirts
flying down the hill to you –

distant, glimmering health;

you, small fig, curled over
in the dark

essence of you
in glass vials

raspberry leaf
liquorice root
stinging nettle
evening primrose

hold you at the back of my iris
clench you in between my thighs

keep you
under my tongue
against the inside of my cheek

like the pink pill
that rolls dissolves
through my tide of blood
and breaks two days later

Nobody

Nobody, here, is a metaphor.
There are no allegories for dead children.

No buzzards that glide and hover silently
above a hospital lit up painfully all night.

No hares sat outside the cemetery gates,
brown, and blending in with all the hedges and ghosts.

No other words for red, black, baby pink, blank.
Or, if there are, none good enough to use.

Or, if there are, none that I've found.
Or, if there are, none that I'll use.

Or, if there are, none that I'll mean.
Or, if there are, none that will hum and vibrate

and pool together to form the vitreous,
none that will whorl and curve into a tragus,

or petrify into metacarpals; fossilize
into tiny brittle fruit and hard roses;

or fly up into the sky and scatter like frightened birds,
or leap into the birds, and crouch there,

in the dark, behind a sparrow's rib-cage,
and become, free from a cold body and closed mouth.

NOTES FOR BROADSHEET POETS

Editor's note: This piece by this eminent composer and conductor seems to fit well into this series as there is a common bond in the composition of every art form, in this case, classical music. As David Jones (who did by hand the logo for *Agenda*) said, all creative artists are 'carpenters of song' and parallels here can be made with composing music and composing poetry.

David Levi is an orchestral conductor and pianist, who divides his time between conducting for opera and ballet companies throughout Europe and directing choral programmes which bring hundreds of adolescents together in Paris and Marseille. He has just brought out the first available recording of the G major cello and piano sonata of the heretofore virtually unknown Russian composer, Leokadiya Kashperova, herself perhaps a Tatiana when she wrote her first compositions. David lives in Southwest France.

Tatiana's Letter

Day's end in Cologne. the laconic light of the Rhineland illuminating the rehearsal stage with its chaotically scattered set pieces put in place, so that we could go through some moments from *Eugene Onegin*. Tomorrow I would conduct my first performance of the Tchaikovsky masterpiece, which runs hot and cold between passion and control.

The singers and stage director had left the stage and I remained alone with the Latvian rehearsal pianist who knew the piece in his fingers, his elbows, his shoulders, and in every organ of his body. Every organ.

Andris waited for the others to leave. Then he squinted up at me and said, with his twisted grin: 'You conductors are all so good, so correct, so precise. But in order to play this music you need to invent it, to let it flow, to let it take you wherever it needs to take you.'

And he started to play the first measures of the introduction, his body bending and convulsing as he squirmed around every contraction and release of harmony, melody and rhythm. I had never heard the music that way. A coldness, which I felt in my heart heretofore regarding the piece, began to melt away. The following evening I stepped in front of the orchestra and just let the opening phrases take us wherever they seemed to need to go, passing through my body, through the bodies of my fellow musicians, shaped by our past experiences, both musical and emotional. I was a lightning rod. I was a conductor.

*

Fast forward twenty-five years. The COVID Pandemic. Theatres worldwide are shuttered. Large orchestras and even larger voices can no longer perform. I can no longer conduct. To keep creative, to keep alive, I come back to *Eugene Onegin* and to Tatiana's letter – Pushkin's text, whispered by countless adolescents who know what it is to give oneself over to love for the first time – that first diary entry, and then that first step to transform the diary entry into a missive to be read by another.

A cellist colleague and I discover a work by a virtually unknown Russian composer who wrote her first sonata for cello and piano at the age of eighteen, publishing it just one year after the première of Tchaikovsky's masterpiece. We decide to record the young Kashperova's Opus 1 No. 1 and also to include our own intimate arrangement for cello and piano of Tatiana's Letter, the love letter which was the first opus of another St. Petersburg adolescent. And yet I never connected my story with Tatiana's until suddenly one morning...

I realized that I had also been Tatiana once.

I was ten years old.

*

It was springtime, with the aroma of rotting leaves emerging from the melting snow. A time for fantasies to begin to be awakened. My older brother knew what love was. I did not. He wrote to his girlfriend of the previous summer. I wrote to a girl named Sallie.

And she wrote back, registering enough encouragement to embolden me in imagining the depth of my attachment to her.

No Tatiana, could have felt more full of confidence than I did.

And so I took the leap, liberated to express my joyful and ever wilder declarations of love. I was bold. I was sensitive. I was a poet. And perhaps I didn't notice that she was not.

After our third exchange of letters, I received the following pungently scented missive.

> *Dear David,*
> *I'm here with my best friend. She and my boyfriend Ted both agree –*
> *you are really queer. So here is a bottle of perfume for you, you queer.*

Within the envelope was an empty flask.

*

As the years went by, I heard that Sallie had become a troubled adolescent, veering towards irresponsible alcohol and drug abuse, and finally finding stability in a born-again Christian community. She married, had several children, suffered physical abuse from her husband.

And I felt vindicated.

And yet the story continued to trouble me. Age forty, I played the Sallie card to my therapist, to explain the reason for certain of my neuroses which, despite two years of therapy, still needed to be treated. There was a silence after I told my story. Voilà, I remember thinking. Now you understand, why I am the way I am.

Silence. And Fernando said: 'And you've never been able to forgive her?' I was astonished. Had he not heard? Had he not understood what she did? Then I shyly looked up at him and the words escaped me: 'You mean I can forgive her?'

Even after years of conducting *Eugene Onegin* and teaching the lyrics of Pushkin's poem – learning to read Cyrillic, incorporating Tchaikovsky's harmonies into my world, allowing their tension to invade me so that I could release them in turn to make way for more tension; taking high-trapeze leaps into musical phrases and knowing that the composer's vision, would buoy me up and toss me into new heights – I had never made the connection between Tatiana's Letter and my own childhood tragedy. After all Art is not therapy. Art is art.

It was the Pandemic that helped me to put the pieces together. Unable to perform and struggling to survive artistically, I had turned to recording. And to Tatiana's Letter. In a moment of existential doubt, the image of my younger self, as sensitive, honest and courageous as Tatiana, presented itself to me – a young boy who took his first steps towards loving and being rejected. The shame I felt at the time may have marked me forever and changed the course of my life. But so it is when the waves of adversity sweep upon us, perhaps to drown us, or perhaps to raise us up to new heights.

And so it is that the crushing Pandemic has lifted me up to remember a lonely girl named Sallie. And Tatiana.

Albert Gelpi

C. Day-Lewis (1904-1972) The 50th anniversary of his death

Albert Gelpi celebrates Cecil Day-Lewis with a special selection of his poems, each of which are introduced by Albert, and can be read in the online web supplement to this issue of *Agenda* www.agendapoetry.co.uk

Albert suggested C Day-Lewis's essay (below) for this Notes for Broadsheet Poets series:

from 'Making a Poem'

'The Gate' is dedicated to Trekkie Parsons, the artist whose small landscape painting, Day-Lewis said, 'held for me a special and mysterious meaning.' This excerpt from a lecture from the mid-sixties, first published in *The Golden Bridle: Selected Prose* (2017), traces the genesis and development of the poem as it searches the painting and arrives at its secret epiphany.

I would like to illustrate with a poem of mine called 'The Gate'. It is one of several written in a state of creative exhilaration stimulated by my first visit to the U.S.A. a few years ago. I have chosen it partly because its data (which are all given in the first six lines of the poem) were apparently simple and straightforward and were already contained within a frame; for the poem arose out of a picture, painted by a friend of mine – a picture to which I responded with pleasure and excitement, but also with a sense that it held for me a special and mysterious meaning I must try to explore through poetry.

The Gate

In the foreground, clots of cream-white flowers (meadow-sweet?
Guelder? Cow parsley?): a patch of green: then a gate
Dividing the green from a brown field; and beyond,
By steps of mustard and sainfoin-pink, the distance
Climbs right-handed away
Up to an olive hilltop and the sky.
The gate it is, dead-centre, ghost-amethyst-hued,
Fastens the whole together like a brooch.
It is all arranged, all there, for the gate's sake
Or for what may come through the gate. But those white flowers,
Craning their necks, putting their heads together,

Like a crowd that holds itself back from surging forward,
Have their own point of balance— poised, it seems,
On the airy brink of whatever it is they await.

And I, gazing over their heads from outside the picture,
Question what we are waiting for: not summer—
Summer is here in charlock, grass and sainfoin.
A human event?— but there's no path to the gate,
Nor does it look as if it was meant to open.
The ghost of one who often came this way
When there was a path? I do not know. But I think,
If I could go deep into the heart of the picture

From the flowers' point of view, all I would ask is
Not that the gate should open, but that it should
Stay there, holding the coloured folds together.
We expect nothing (the flowers might add), we only
Await: this pure awaiting—
It is the kind of worship we are taught.

This poem was written more or less straight ahead: more often I compose a bit here, a bit there, like a painter. The first stanza objectively sets out the facts – the colour and detail of the pictured landscape. In the second stanza, the eye pans up to its dominant features – the flowers in the foreground, the gate in the centre focusing the whole landscape together. At this point I still had no idea why the picture had such attractive mystery for me, or what it was trying to convey. However, in this second stanza I concentrated upon its main features subjectively – the central mystery, and my sense that the foreground flowers stood in an attentive pose, waiting for something to happen.

But I still had not discovered the theme of the growing poem. So, in stanza three, I tried putting a number of questions to the picture: just what are the flowers, and myself the outside observer, waiting for? Several possible answers were given, and each of them in turn rejected; but the first seven lines are constructed out of this series of rejections, in such a way that their logical negatives create something emotionally positive. And then, at last, I saw what the landscape – and the poem – were saying to me. I saw it by moving from outside the picture and looking at the gate 'from the flowers' point of view.' In my tiny way I had done what Copernicus did when, with a superb imaginative leap, leaving the earth and placing himself in the sun, he found that the orbits of the planets looked simpler from that point of view.

What the picture was saying to me, I discovered, is first that the flowers expect nothing, their task being one of 'pure awaiting', a kind of worship; and second, that they (and I) are not concerned with a divine revelation (the gate opening), but only that the gate should stay there – in other words, that we should retain the sense of some Power at the centre of things, holding them together. This idea is foreshadowed (line eight) in purely visual or aesthetic terms: it was not till I reached the final stanza that I became aware of its deeper significance and realized that the poem was a religious poem. It is also, obviously, the poem of an agnostic – one who is, in a sense, 'outside the picture' – but an agnostic whose upbringing was Christian: the 'olive hilltop', with its echo of Mount Olivet, may conceivably have started the poem in the religious direction which, unforeseen by me, it was to take; and the 'ghost-amethyst' colour of the gate certainly led me along to 'The ghost of one who often came this way', i.e. the once-felt presence of deity in the human scene.

A few technical points: the poem had no end-rhymes, but the two most important words in it rhyme and are repeated – 'gate' six times, 'wait' ('await', 'awaiting') four times. The stanzas are carefully organized, the first corresponding metrically with the last, the second with the third: the pause between third and fourth stanza, which should be observed in reading the poem aloud throws the greatest possible emphasis on 'From the flowers' point of view', highlighting the change of position which is to reveal the theme. Finally, the rhythms are as flexible as I could make them, within a regular metre, so as to reflect the inquiring and tentative nature of the poem's thought-process.

Talking about the poem in this detached way, I have given the impression perhaps that a poem 'writes itself'. Nothing could be further from the truth – in my case, at any rate. Certainly, in the first phase of composition, the 'fishing' phase, the intellect is relatively inactive; one accepts, in a trance-like state, everything that comes up. But there follows a phase of the most arduous intellectual activity, when the gathered material has to be criticized in the light of the growing poem and of whatever inkling I may have about its theme. Since the two phases constantly overlap, it is almost impossible to give a blow-by-blow commentary on the making of a poem. All I can say is that my mind moves gradually over from passive to active, as it tries to per- form the two functions of making and of exploring.

James Roberts

Leleka

We wait for the white birds
all stilts and sticks
ripped cloth and clatter
their fingers dipped in our soot
their feet in our blood
heading home to our roofs
where we fixed wooden wheels
as foundations for their homes.
They'll gather splinters from trees
and make a rickety bone pile
with a preened hollow to hold
their silk-skinned newborns.
They bring us luck, fine weather.
We look up from our woes.
The wind will blow them here soon
as we migrate anywhere else
our convoys leagues long
the nests we've left behind
throwing up flocks of sparks.

Note:
The stork is called Leleka in Ukraine. White storks migrate there in March each year.

David Pollard

Madrigal for a Lost Soul

Its wings as wide as shadows
the great bird of mists sets sail on night seas
along the gusting air that is too ghostly wild
for the black heart within the eye
to half see what the mist unfocuses
and blinds the wild infirmities

threatening the nakedness of almost night
just as it fails and falls.

From the veined branches
come the scattered caws
after the thunder passes
and the clouds lowering
with wings that flap like devils.

In the mind's eye
and glimmer from behind the glass
hung opposite the window
another one than ought
seems to stare back
surprised at seeing in me
the in between
of so much space reversed.

Wild Horses of Chernobyl

Anon

Where are you, wild horses of Chernobyl?

Did you think it thunder: the rumbling
of Russian tanks in the No Man's Land
now a nature reserve – as the earth
churned by their heavy tracks put you
at a renewed risk of contamination?
Maybe you sensed the sudden levels
of radiation climbing the trees
sky-high, and warned the wolves, bison,
brown bears, elk and lynx, all birdsong
on hold. Ghosts in a ghost town,
whited out by blizzards, you shelter
at times with dogs, once pets,
in ground floors of derelict office blocks,
looking out onto woods red-dead
from dust. I imagine you, wild horses,
pushing through walls of deserted kindergartens,
picking up limbs between your teeth

to put back onto cherished, abandoned dolls –.
spooking at memories of dizzy horses
on carrousels, plastic peeling off.

Come, wild horses of Chernobyl,
gallop away through Pripyat, Skavutych –
to Kyiv where wide eyed children, vulnerable
as you, will climb onto your backs
from their mothers' arms, for transport
to the Carpathian mountains. There
neither they, nor you, need ever be ghosts
again in that place where you could die
at a touch. With coats still the colour
of the Gobi desert you came from, and manes
stiff as brushes to sweep missiles from skies,
the Spring will be more than a glimpse
of green from crevices in a mildewed hotel
once filled with guests.
        And O, wild horses, may you
breed fillies and colts that whinny
through the valleys of our hearts and minds
for the innocents sacrificed everywhere.

W S Milne

The Night of the Murdered Poets

*i.m. Peretz Markish, David Hofstein, Itzik Feffer and
Leib Kvitko, Yiddish poets executed in Lubyanka Prison,
Moscow, on 12 August 1952.*

The hour of night comes quieter,
sadder… Death has already touched us.
We will never again knock on your door,
we will never again gather at your house –
but we will enter your hearts
now – open to everyone, accessible to everyone,
like the singing cricket, like the forest welcoming,
like the face of free waters – like the sun.

Biographies

Shanta Acharya, born and educated in India, won a scholarship to Oxford, where she was among the first batch of women admitted to Worcester College. A recipient of the Violet Vaughan Morgan Fellowship, she was awarded the Doctor of Philosophy for her work on Ralph Waldo Emerson. She was a Visiting Scholar in the Department of English and American Literature and Languages at Harvard University. The author of twelve books, her publications range from poetry, literary criticism and fiction to finance. Her most recent publications are *What Survives Is The Singing* (Indigo Dreams Publishing, 2020) and *Imagine: New and Selected Poems* (HarperCollins Publishing, 2017). www.shanta-acharya.com

Timothy Adès is a rhyming translator-poet with books from French, two of them from Agenda Editions, and from Spanish, and awards.for Cassou, Desnos, Hugo, and Alfonso Reyes. He rewrote Shakespeare's 154 Sonnets without using letter E. He translates Brecht, Ricarda Huch, Sikelianós, and many more, and is one of *Agenda*'s Trustees.

Linda Anderson published her first poetry collection, *The Station Before*, with Pavilion Poetry in 2020. It was shortlisted for the Seamus Heaney first collection prize. She has also published numerous critical books and essays including, *Elizabeth Bishop: Lines of Connection* (EUP, 2013).

Kate Ashton was born in Beith and returned to live in the Highlands of Scotland in 2003, having spent 25 years in the Netherlands. She writes narrative non-fiction and translates from Dutch and Frisian. Her poems and reviews have appeared in UK magazines and webzines including *THE SHOp*, *Glasgow Review of Books*, *Agenda, Shearsman, Shadowtrain, Causeway, Molly Bloom, londongrip.com* and *Long Poem Magazine*. A pamphlet, *The Concourse of Virgins* was published by Lapwing in 2012, and her first collection, *Who by Water*, came out from Shearsman Books in 2016. She is currently working on a second collection.

Elizabeth Barton read English at Cambridge, after which she worked as a teacher and reviewer. Her poems have appeared in magazines including *Agenda, Acumen, The High Window, The Frogmore Papers, Orbis* and *South*. She is Stanza Rep for Mole Valley Poets and enjoys leading Ecopoetry workshops. Her pamphlet, *If Grief were a Bird*, will be published by *Agenda* later this year.

Matthew Barton is the editor of *Raceme* online poetry journal. He has had several poetry collections published, the latest of which is reviewed in this issue by Elizabeth Barton.

John Bourke has published many poems in newspapers and periodicals both in Ireland and England. He has taught in University College Cork, as well as in London from 1988 to 2004. He is currently teaching English Language and Literature in a large Secondary school in West Limerick, Ireland.

Diana Cant is a child psychotherapist living in rural Kent. She has an MA in Poetry from Newcastle University / The Poetry School. Her poems have been published in various anthologies and magazines. In 2021 she was voted Canterbury People's Poet, was commended in the Hippocrates Prize and was a winner in the Spelt competition. Her pamphlet, *Student Bodies 1968*, was published in 2020 by Clayhanger Press, and her second pamphlet, *At Risk – the lives some children live*, was published by Dempsey and Windle in 2021.

Peter Carpenter 's poems have appeared in many literary journals including the *TLS* and *Poetry Review* and have been widely anthologised, in Bloodaxe's *Lifesaving Poems*, for example. There have been six previous collections including *Just Like That*, a New and Selected Poems. A pamphlet is due from Mariscat in late 2022, and a full collection with Smith|Doorstop in 2023. He teaches creative writing for the Arvon Foundation and has worked at many universities including Cambridge, Exeter, Reading and Warwick (where he worked as a Visiting Fellow for the Writing Programme). His chapter on the teaching of creative writing appeared in the OUP Companion *to British and Irish Poetry*. He co-directs Worple Press and lives in Suffolk

Martin Caseley regularly contributes essays, articles and poems to *Agenda, PN Review,* and *The Countryman*. Recently he has written on Louis MacNeice, teasels, The Pop Group, Philip Larkin, Richard Jefferies and ancient milestones. He continues to explore a wide range of interests from his base in Norfolk and also reviews books for the *International Times* and *Stride* Magazine websites.

Belinda Cooke's recent poetry collections include *Stem* (The High Window Press, 2019) and *Days of the Shorthanded Shovelists* (forthcoming from Salmon Poetry). Her translations from the Russian and Kazakh include *Kulager Ilias Jansugurov* (Kazakh N.T. A., 2018); *Forms of Exile: Poems of Marina Tsvetaeva* (The High Window Press, 2019); (et al) *Contemporary Kazakh Poetry* (C.U.P, 2019). Her memoir of her mother: *From the Back of Beyond to Westland Row: an Irish Woman's Story* is also forthcoming this summer from The High Window Press.

David Cooke was born in Reading in 1953, although his family comes from the West of Ireland. He won a Gregory award as a student and has since published eight collections of his work, the most recent of which is *Sicilian Elephants* (Two Rivers Press, 2021). He is also the founding editor of the online journal *The High Window*.

Martyn Crucefix's recent publications: *Cargo of Limbs* (Hercules Editions, 2019) and *The Lovely Disciplines* (Seren, 2017). *These Numbered Days*, translations of poems by Peter Huchel (Shearsman, 2019) won the Schlegel-Tieck Translation Prize, 2020. A Rilke *Selected* will be published by Pushkin Press in 2023 and a translation of Lutz Seiler's essays, *Sundays I Thought of God* will be published by And Other Stories. Royal Literary Fund Fellow at The British Library, he blogs on poetry, translation and teaching at http:// www.martyncrucefix.com

Peter Dale is the author of many collections of poetry published mainly by Agenda Editions and Anvil Press. He is also a translator e.g. of Villon, Superveille, Dante, and he has recently started writing crime novels. He was for many years Associate Editor of Agenda, with William Cookson. He now lives in Wales.

Hilary Davies' most recent publications are as a co-translator of Yves Bonnefoy's *Collected Prose*, (Carcanet, 2020) and co-editor of *Prophetic Witness. The Re-Imagining of the World,* (Routledge, 2020). She has been a Royal Literary Fund Fellow at King's College, London and the British Library, and is a former Chairman of the Poetry Society.

John F. Deane was born on Achill Island off the west coast of Ireland. He is founder of Poetry Ireland, Ireland's national poetry society, and its journal *The Poetry Ireland Review*. A new collection *Dear Pilgrims* appeared from Carcanet in 2018 and a collection of poems set on Achill Island with paintings by John Behan, *Achill: The Island* published by Currach Press also appeared in 2018. In 2016 Deane was the Teilhard de Chardin Fellow in Catholic Studies in Loyola University, Chicago and taught a course in poetry. In 2019 he was visiting poet in Notre Dame University in Indiana. His new collection of poems, *Naming of the Bones* (Carcanet, 2021), is reviewed in this issue of *Agenda*.

Greg Delanty's latest collection of poems is *No More Time*. Other recent books are *Selected Delanty* *(*Selected and introduced by Archie Burnett) and *The Greek Anthology Book XVI* (Oxford Poets, Carcanet Press, UK – titled *Book Seventeen* in US (LSU Press) He has received many awards, including a Guggenheim for poetry. In March of 2021 he was awarded The David Ferry and Ellen LaForge Poetry Prize for his body of work. He teaches at Saint Michael's College, Vermont. Delanty's papers up to 2010 have been acquired by the National Library of Ireland and from 2010-2015 at University College, Cork.

Albert Gelpi is the William Robertson Coe Professor of American Literature emeritus, at Stanford University. He and Day-Lewis became friends during Day-Lewis's year at Harvard as the Norton Professor of Poetry. He wrote a critical study of Day-Lewis's poetry, *Living in Time* (1998), and edited, with Bernard O'Donoghue, a volume of Day-Lewis's prose, *The Golden Bridle* (2017).

John Griffin was born and raised in Tipperary, Ireland, and emigrated to the USA in his teens, where he subsequently read for his BA, MFA, MA, and PhD, specializing in German Idealist Philosophy as it laid the groundwork for British Romantic Aesthetics, especially in the writings of Samuel Taylor Coleridge, whose proposed though unwritten *Opus Maximus* was the subject of his thesis. He has published poems & essays in literary journals – *Agenda, The Esthetic Apostle, The Charles River Review, The Common, The Little Star Poetry Magazine, Hawk & Whippoorwill,* and *Planisphere Quarterly,* as well as 2 chapbooks, *After Love* and *Absences ~ A Sequence*. He now lives in Riyadh, Saudi Arabia, where he works at King Saud University.

Jeremy Hooker was born in Hampshire but has spent most of his working life in Wales. He has published two *Selected Poems*, with Enitharmon and Shearsman respectively, and his books of essays, on poetry, nature, and painting, and published journals include: *Poetry of Place*, *Imagining Wales*, *Ditch Vision*, *Art of Seeing*, *Welsh Journal* and *Openings: A European Journal*. His BBC 3 feature *A Map of David Jones* was first broadcast in 1995. He is a Fellow of The Learned Society of Wales and Emeritus Professor of the University of South Wales.

Timothy Houghton's *The Internal Distance (Selected Poems 1989-2012)* appeared in a bilingual (Italian/English) edition from the Italian press Hebenon/Mimesis Edizioni in 2015. The book was presented in Florence at the Museo Casa di Dante. He has worked at Yaddo, MacDowell, and Hawthornden Castle. His recent book is *Where the Lighthouse Begins* (Salmon Poetry, 2020). He has published in *Agenda* and numerous other journals in the U.K. and Ireland. He is a field trip coordinator for Audubon.

W.D. Jackson's five books and a pamphlet are all parts of his work-in-progress, *Then and Now*, on the subject of the individual and his or her place in history. The most recent of them, *Opus 3* (Shoestring Press, 2018), was a *TLS* Book of the Year.

Dr Patrick Lodge is an Irish/Welsh poet whose work has been published, anthologised and translated in several countries and has read, by invitation, at poetry festivals in the UK, Ireland, Kosovo and Italy. He has been successful in several international poetry competitions. In 2021 he won the Poetry On The Lake short story competition. Patrick reviews for several poetry magazines and has judged international poetry competitions. His collections, *An Anniversary of Flight*, *Shenanigans* and *Remarkable Occurrences* were published by the Yorkshire publisher, Valley Press. He is currently working on a fourth collection provisionally entitled *Arkana*.

Jane Lovell is an award-winning poet whose work focuses on our relationship with the planet and its wildlife. She has been widely published in journals and anthologies in the UK and US. Jane has won the Flambard Prize, the Wigtown Prize, the Geoff Stevens Memorial Prize and this year's Ginkgo Prize. Her new collection, *The God of Lost Ways*, is published by Indigo Dreams Press and is reviewed in this issue of *Agenda*.

Merryn MacCarthy grew up near Dublin and in Southern England. A career teacher, she was for many years Head of English in East Sussex. Her poems have been published in the Irish press and in the UK, including *English*, Sussex University Press and *Agenda*. Her collection *Playing Truant* came out in Agenda Editions in 2010. Her bilingual edition, *Seeking the Mountains*,2016, was inspired by retiring to South-West France, where she has also been published by *The French Literary Review*.

Caroline Maldonado is a poet and translator. Translations from Italian include *Your call keeps us awake (2013)*, *Isabella (2019)*; *Liminal* (2020) and forthcoming *Nadir* (2022) all published by Smokestack Books. Her own poems can be found in *What they say in Avenale* (Indigo Dreams Publishing 2014) and forthcoming *Faultlines (*Vole Books 2022).

W S Milne was born in Aberdeen in 1953 and now lives in Surrey. Having worked for many years as a teacher in Further Education, he now writes full time. He reviews regularly for *Agenda*, and for other magazines. He has published several books of poetry in Scots, a translation of Aeschylus' *Agamemnon* (in Scots) and a critical study of the English poet Geoffrey Hill. Five Scottish plays of his have been published in *Lallans* magazine with a sixth coming out in the next issue.

Annemarie Ní Churreáin is a poet from Donegal in northwest Ireland. She is author of *Bloodroot* (Doire Press 2017), *Town* (The Salvage Press, 2018) and *The Poison Glen* (The Gallery Press, 2021). Ní Churreáin is a recipient of The Next Generation Award from the Irish Arts Council and a co-recipient of The Markievicz Award. She has been Writer-In-Residence at Akadamie Schloss Solitude in Germany, Jack Kerouac House in Florida & Centre Culturel Irlandais, Paris. Ní Churreáin is 2022 Guest Editor *The Stony Thursday Book* Edition 44 and *The Cormorant* Issue 7. Visit www.studiotwentyfive.com

Mary O'Donnell is an established poet, novelist and short-story writer living in Ireland. Her eighth collection *Massacre of the Birds* was published in 2020 by Salmon and is reviewed in this issue of *Agenda*. Previous work includes *Those April Fevers* and *The Ark Builders* from Ark Publications. Her most recent fiction is the 2018 collection of linked stories, *Empire*. Essays on her work appeared in the Peter Lang published volume *Giving Shape to the Moment: The Art of Mary O'Donnell*, also in 2018. She is a member of Ireland's affiliation of artists, Aosdana.

David Pollard is the author of several prize-winning collections of poems. *Bird of Oblivion* will be brought out by Agenda Editions in July 2022.

James Roberts is a writer and artist based in the Welsh Borders. His poems have been published widely and he is a long term contributor to *Agenda*. He releases much of his work via his own imprint Night River Wood. A non-fiction book, *Two Lights*, will be published by September Publishing in Spring 2023.

Robert Selby's debut collection, *The Coming-Down Time*, was published by Shoestring Press in 2020. *The Kentish Rebellion*, a book-length sequence set during the English Civil War, is forthcoming from Shoestring in 2022. His poems and reviews have appeared in *PN Review, Poetry London, The Spectator*, the *Times Literary Supplement*, and elsewhere.

Gerard Smyth was born in Dublin in 1951 and has published ten collections of poetry, the most recent of which are *The Sundays of Eternity* (reviewed in this issue) and *A Song of Elsewhere* (both Dedalus Press). *The Yellow River* (with artwork by Seán McSweeney) was published by Solstice Arts Centre. He is a member of Aosdána (Ireland's affiliation of artists) and Poetry Editor of *The Irish Times*.

Duncan Sprott is (still) writing a novel about Kleopatra, to be published by Faber.

Will Stone is a poet, essayist and literary translator. His first poetry collection, *Glaciation* (Salt, 2007), won the international Glen Dimplex Award˙ for poetry in 2008. His subsequent collections *Drawing in Ash* (Salt, 2011) *The Sleepwalkers* (Shearsman, 2016) and *The Slowing Ride* (Shearsman, 2020) were critically appraised. Will's published translations from French and German include works by Georg Trakl, Stefan Zweig, Joseph Roth, Rainer Maria Rilke, Gérard de Nerval, Emile Verhaeren and Georges Rodenbach. His most recent published translations were *Poems to Night* by Rainer Maria Rilke (Pushkin, 2020) – reviewed here – and *Encounters and Destinies – A Farewell to Europe*, by Zweig (Pushkin, 2020). Two first English translations from the French are forthcoming: *Nietzsche in Italy* by Guy de Pourtalès (Pushkin, July 2022) and *Letters around a Garden* by Rilke (Seagull Books, 2023). Will has contributed to a number of other publications including *The TLS, Apollo Magazine, The Spectator, RA Magazine, Irish Pages, Modern Poetry in Translation, The London Magazine and Poetry Review*.

Peter Weltner was raised in northern New Jersey and Piedmont North Carolina and educated at Hamilton College (A.B.) and Indiana University (Ph.D.). For thirty seven years, he taught Renaissance, modern, and contemporary poetry and prose in the English Department of San Francisco State. He has published seven books of fiction, including *The Risk of His Music* and *The Return of What's Been Lost*, and fifteen books or chapbooks of poetry, the most recent *Scrapbook Mappings of My Country* and *Woods and the City*. With his husband of 36 years and their lab-mix Robbie, he lives in San Francisco near the western edge of Golden Gate Park by the Pacific.

Patrick Wright's poetry collection, *Full Sight Of Her* (Eyewear, 2020) is reviewed here. He has been shortlisted for the Bridport Prize, and teaches English and Creative Writing at the Open University. He is also about to complete a PhD in Creative Writing, on the ekphrasis of modern and contemporary art, supervised by Siobhan Campbell and Jane Yeh.

SPECIAL FEATURE

C. Day-Lewis (1904-1972)

A SELECTION OF POEMS FOR THE 50th ANNIVERSARY OF HIS DEATH

Selection of poems by this undeservedly neglected poet by Professor Albert Gelpi with a short introduction by him on each poem

More poems by some poets in this issue and fresh voices:

David Harsent
Peter Weltner
Jane Lovell
Peter Carpenter
Timothy Adès
Bernadette Gallagher
Greg Delanty
Erica Collier
Elizabeth Barton
Diana Cant
Hilary Davies
Kate Ashton
Shanta Acharya
Timothy Houghton
Omar Sabbagh
Christopher Nield
Indran Amirthanayagam
Colin Bancroft

Timothy Adès: Horace's Phantom Hero

More poems from **Marina Tsvetaeva**'s *Wires* translated by Belinda Cooke

Essays/reviews

Nicole Waldner: *'The silence of the hook is what you must note.'* János Pilinszky's Centenary (1921-1981)

W D Jackson: Rilke's Grave Re-visited

W S Milne: The Poetry of Jane Kenyon

Paul Dean: Thom Gunn: Metre, Movement, Meaning

James Harpur: Mick Evans
– Light Airs

Omar Sabbagh: Mirrors and Carnivals – on Abhay K's *The Alphabets of Latin America* (Bloomsbury)

John O'Donoghue: Michael McCarthy
– Like a tree cut back

W S Milne: Anthony Mair
– A Suitcase Filled With Hope
Mara Bergman
– The Night We Were Dylan Thomas

Merryn Williams: Billy Collins
– Whale Day
Elizabeth Cook *– When I kiss the sky*
Denise Riley *– Lurex*

David Cooke: *Apathy is Out / Ni Ceadmhach Neamhshuim, Selected Poems / Rogha Dánta* by Seán Ó Ríordain translated by Greg Delanty

Featured artists: **Mary Harris**
Johnny Marsh

A bouquet of paintings by artists from Ukraine selected by **Ursula O'Reilly Traynor.**